COLLECTOR'S ENCYCLOPEDIA OF

BAUER
POTTERY

IDENTIFICATION & VALUES

JACK CHIPMAN

COLLECTOR BOOKS
A Division of Schroeder Publishing Co., Inc.

The current values in this book should be used only as a guide. They are not intended to set prices, which vary from one section of the country to another. Auction prices as well as dealer prices vary greatly and are affected by condition and demand. Neither the author nor the publisher assumes responsibility for any losses which might be incurred as a result of consulting this guide.

Cover design: Beth Summers
Book layout: Jack Chipman, Victoria Damrel, Karen Geary

Searching For A Publisher?

We are always looking for people knowledgeable within their fields. If you feel that there is a real need for a book on your collectible subject and have a large comprehensive collection, contact Collector Books.

Collector Books
P.O. Box 3009
Paducah, KY 42002-3009
www.collectorbooks.com

Jack Chipman
P.O. Box 1079
Venice, CA 90294
(for autographed books)

CONTENTS

DEDICATION

This book is dedicated to the memory of Buddy Wilson. For those who don't know, Buddy was the visionary Southern California collector/dealer who cleared the path that so many of us now pursue. In the early seventies, at the unheralded dawning of the collectibles era, he opened "Olde Stuff" in Venice featuring Bauer and other archetypal California potteries. He later relocated to upscale Melrose Avenue in Hollywood as "Buddy's." Buddy infused Bauer collecting with an unmatched intensity of passion, purpose, and dedication. He is missed!

John Andrew Bauer and family, circa 1895, about a decade after the founding of the Bauer Pottery in Paducah, Kentucky.

ACKNOWLEDGMENTS

Most things in life are the result of combined effort, and this book was no exception. So many generous people have contributed that I'm truly at a loss for words to adequately acknowledge them. In the long (and ultimately futile) attempt to justify my obsession with Bauer pottery, I have uncovered a wealth of information about the company and its able personnel. Most of this knowledge has come from people closely associated with the business. Without them a factual Bauer account could not have been written.

I want to thank Victor F. Houser for enduring numerous personal interviews and telephone follow-ups over the years. His informed insight and painstaking recollections have given the Bauer story its remarkable historical perspective. Many additional insights into the Bauer operations, both in Los Angeles and Atlanta, were furnished by John Herbert Brutsche. He was very generous with his time in providing me with historical reminiscences and in lending me pottery and important printed materials. My sincere appreciation to Brenda Johnson Escoto for the detailed histories of her grandfather, Fred Johnson, and her father, Jim Johnson. The data and photographs she freely supplied have added greatly to the record of these key personnel in addition to others in the organization. I'm grateful to Ray Murray, a very talented artist who died on December 15, 1996, for recounting his brief but significant association with the business. Many thanks to Marnie Sheahan Paulus for providing the photograph of the Bauer family (she is the granddaughter of Mayme Bauer), to Vicky Ipsen Grage for supplying photographs and facts concerning her grandfather, Louis Ipsen. Lastly, I wish to thank John Miali for chronicling his and father Gaetano (Guy) Miali's affiliation with the company, and Lance J. Valenzuela for lending the photograph of his grandfather, Louis Kopecky, and his Southgate pottery yard that featured Bauer pottery.

No book of this nature would be comprehensive without the photographer's skill and inventiveness — only a few of the fine qualities of my principal photographer, Victoria Damrel. Victoria utilized her considerable talents and experience in art documentation while working on this project. In addition her computer skills facilitated the layout of text and accompanying visual materials. I am grateful beyond words. In a few instances it became necessary to enlist the services of location photographers. Therefore, a number of supporting cameramen must be acknowledged (in alphabetical order): Adam Anik, Dragon Rock, New York; Dennis Ashlock, Walnut Creek, California; Cliff Coles, Eugene, Oregon; and Chris Witzke, Sacramento, California. I am indebted to all of them and where possible have noted their special contributions as they appear throughout the book.

The following Bauer dealers and/or collectors responded to my pricing survey: Frank Baldizan, Ken Bauer, Jeffrey Dangermond, Jimm Edgar, James Elliot, Glenna Ford, Mark Gearhart, April Hampton, Jeff Martinez, Doug Stanton, Betsy Stubbs, Marc Tisdale, Michael Verlangieri, and Brian Young. (States represented were California, Illinois, Oregon, Texas, and Washington.) Those who supplied specialized evaluations or augmented their personal loans of pottery with pricing information included Jimm Edgar, Carl Gibbs, Jr., Tim Lukaszewski and Paul Preston, Ken Stalcup, Doug Stanton, Mitch Tuchman, and Michael Verlangieri. My sincere appreciation to all who helped with the pricing of Bauer pottery. This was certainly the most challenging aspect of the book.

There were a number of others who assisted with important tasks. Jimm Edgar provided leads in locating elusive items, Glenna Ford helped me with fundraising, Donna Yarrell helped in various ways, including writing "About the Author," and Lou Volse went "which hunting": he edited the text and proofread the finished manuscript. Although the Bauer collectors who entrusted portions of their personal collections during the photography sessions comprise a separate list (see "Contributors"), I want to acknowledge those who "went the extra mile" by hauling (often over long distances) boxes of fragile pottery to my studio: Shari Green, John Hoover, Tim Lukaszewski and Paul Preston, Tom Rogers, and Doug Stanton.

Lastly, a very special thanks to Brian Young and Shari Green for sharing hard-to-find Bauer documents, and to Joseph Smith (I dub thee St. Joseph) and his partner, John Carlotti, for culling through their extensive Bauer collection for items to fill last-minute gaps in the book's photo spreads.

J.A. Bauer Pottery Company display at Los Angeles Hardware Show, 1936.

CONTRIBUTORS

Many people entrusted prized examples to our care during the lengthy process of documenting the wide range of Bauer pottery. Others, in far-flung locales, opted to have pieces from their collections professionally photographed at studios closer to home. I am indebted to each and every one for their ardent participation in this endeavor:

- Doug Albacete, Vacaville, CA
- Jeffrey Bilson & Marcie Begleiter, Los Angeles, CA
- Zack Boles, Sacramento, CA
- Melissa & William Bolinger III, Bakersfield, CA
- John Herbert Brutsche, Newport Beach, CA
- Jeffrey Dangermond, San Francisco, CA
- Dean Dozer, West Hollywood, CA
- Jimm Edgar, Oakland, CA
- Glenna Ford, Ford's Antiques, Pasadena, CA
- Shari Greene, Topanga, CA
- John Hoover, Laguna Beach, CA
- Jeff Martinez, Pasadena Antiques Center, Pasadena, CA
- Barbara Molinaro, El Segundo, CA
- Jack Moore, Jack Moore Arts & Crafts, Pasadena, CA
- Naomi Murdach, Naomi's, San Francisco, CA
- Bobbi Murphy, Park Place Antiques, Fullerton, CA
- Dennis J. Mykytyn, Chappaqua, NY
- Paul Preston & Tim Lukaszewski, Berkeley, CA
- Tom Rogers, San Diego, CA
- John Ryan, Venice, CA
- Ben "Bear" Sawtelle, Bear Cave, Oakland, CA
- Alvin Schell, New York, NY
- Bob Schmid, Chino Hills, CA
- Joseph Smith & John Carlotti, Joseph's Antiques, Coburg, OR
- Steve Soukup, Van Nuys, CA
- Doug Stanton, San Diego, CA
- Bill Stern, Los Angeles, CA
- Judy J. Stangler, Culver City, CA
- Baron Stoelting, Palmdale, CA
- Bill Straus, New York, NY
- Nancy Thomas, Los Angeles, CA
- Marc Tisdale, Marc's, Pasadena, CA
- Mitch Tuchman, Los Angeles, CA
- Marilyn Webb, Redondo Beach, CA
- Mark Wiskow & Susan Strommer, San Francisco, CA

INTRODUCTION: Collecting Bauer

Of course a lot of these pretty bright colors had been used for hundreds of years on artware and tiles, but apparently nobody had thought of putting these kinds of glazes on dishes...

— Victor Houser

Where to begin? I guess the beginning for me was the summer of 1973 when I attended my very first flea market. It was an eagerly awaited weekly affair that took place on an unpaved lot in the delightful community of Sausalito, just north of San Francisco. I went along to help a friend who was selling off an accumulation of stuff — mostly used clothing and household items she no longer used or wanted. After the horde of dealers had descended and swiftly siphoned off the cream of her discards, I decided to venture out on my own to see what flea marketing was all about. I was pretty green at the time and definitely inexperienced in this specialized activity.

All I remember is being drawn over and over to stacks of brightly colored dishes. I finally got nerve enough to ask one of the seasoned dealers (a "reg") just what was grabbing my attention. "Oh those plates are Fiesta, and some of them are Bauer. They were made in L. A. in the thirties." My interest was piqued and I purchased some of his pottery that day — a few pieces of Fiesta ware, clearly marked on the bottom, and maybe one or two unmarked Bauer dinner plates. It would be a stretch to recall exactly what I ended up taking home, but I do know the experience was a turning point in my life.

Before too long I joined the ranks of the "regs" myself and was one of the early arrivals every Sunday, later setting-up and selling my finds: Bauer, Fiesta, McCoy, and other interesting examples of

A view of Jimm Edgar and Bettie Dakota Edgar's Bauer Pottery collection.

America's pottery past. And the pickings were pretty good in those heady early days of buying/selling collectibles. There were very few guide books then so dealers and collectors were basically on their own. Like everyone else I soon put together an impressive collection of McCoy pottery, later graduating to the bigger Ohio names like Roseville, Rookwood, Weller, and so on. But the real turning point occurred after I moved back home to Los Angeles in 1976. Then and there I made the fateful decision to focus my collecting efforts solely on Bauer and other potteries of my native state.

Today I'm less green in my incessant pursuit of California Pottery. Meanwhile Bauer has become one of the enchanted names in the panoply of collectible American Pottery. It has been the subject of numerous articles, books, and exhibitions in art galleries and museums on the West Coast. This is the second Bauer reference guide that I have put together, the first being *The Complete Collectors Guide to Bauer Pottery*, originally published in 1982 with collaborator, Judy Stangler. The success of that first self-published edition led to a second printing by Jo-D Books of Stamford, Connecticut, in 1986, along with an update of the supplemental *Bauer Pottery Price Guide*. These books have been out-of-print for sometime, but information seekers and Bauer aficionados still persist in their search, paying surprisingly high prices to acquire them.

Because there has not been an update of the *Bauer Pottery Price Guide* since 1986, values for common to rare items have increased dramatically. Yes the stakes are much higher today, which is one reason I have resisted this task for so long. Another reason is that I have not been actively selling Bauer Pottery in recent years. Therefore I have turned to active dealers for assistance. The pricing information contained in this book is a median of the input I have received, mitigated by my own experience of shopping the California market for items to add to my personal collection. Dealers in many parts of the country responded to my questionnaire, so prices are not based solely on the California market but reflect the growing interest in Bauer throughout the country.

My original (impossible) goal of including everything that Bauer ever made was naturally not realized, but I did make the attempt. And I was amazed to find that even after so long in the field I was face to face with Bauer pieces I had never seen before. So who knows what is still out there waiting to be uncovered? This aspect, of course, is one of the greatest thrills of collecting — making that once-in-a- lifetime discovery.

BAUER: A Short History

J. A. Bauer

Roots of the enterprise known as the J. A. Bauer Pottery extend more than half way across the country from Los Angeles to Paducah, Kentucky. There, in 1885, John Andrew (Andy) Bauer, the son of German immigrants, established his Paducah Pottery by buying out the owner of an existing ceramics business. It was a large and diversified operation that supplied the region with sanitary stoneware, "stoneware specialties," and red clay flower pots. Much of the trade was in whiskey jugs for the local distilleries. But other jugs, growlers (beer containers), mugs, bean pots, mixing bowls, chamber pots, water coolers, and the like were produced. Local clays were utilized almost exclusively. Bauer even owned his own clay bed, which was situated a short distance from the physical plant. It was a successful operation by any measure. So much so that the proprietor was able to spend the winters with his family in sunny Southern California, where Andy Bauer found relief from an asthma condition. By 1909, he had made the decision to relocate his business to Los Angeles.

The J. A. Bauer Pottery Company was officially established in Los Angeles in 1910, although construction of the plant had begun the previous year. It was situated in the Lincoln Heights district, about half way between the city's hub and the sleepy suburb of Pasadena. The location, at 415-421 West Avenue 33 (near the corner of Lacy Street), was no accident. Andy Bauer had selected his new pottery's address with considerable care.

The site chosen for the new pottery was a thriving ceramics district with numerous plants already in operation, including nearby Pacific Clay Products. Rail transportation was right at hand for easy shipping of materials and finished goods. Locally abundant natural gas provided fuel for the plant's four massive periodic ("beehive") kilns. The same kilns were later equipped to burn oil in the event that gas became scarce.

Initially the same products offered to the public in Paducah were produced in Los Angeles. Some of these included butter churns, pickle jars, pitchers, chamber pots, mixing bowls, and nappies. Many of the familiar crocks and jugs that were used as containers for commercial food and beverage products back in Kentucky were made available in the new land. Southern California was still a semi-rural region at this time, so many farm-related articles were also manufactured. Still, the bestselling product of the new enterprise was the humble yet essential red clay flower pot. Although these too had been a sustaining product in earlier years, orders were received from the Los Angeles area nursery trade in unprecedented numbers. And Bauer was quick to respond, establishing the new business as the leading local source for these much needed items. Not only were they used by the average home planter in significant numbers, but commercial growers seemed to need them in droves.

As time went by, designs the company called "fancy" were added to the flower pot line. Some of these can be seen in the catalogs of the teens and twenties. But who was designing all these goods? It would have been prudent for Andy Bauer to bring with him a capable modeler and mold maker from Paducah. And he may have. But the idiosyncrasies of a new region demanded a new approach, or at least someone in the capacity of designer who would be able to respond to the demands of a unique and fast-growing region.

It was Louis Ipsen who filled the bill, and was hired soon after the business was established, perhaps as early as 1912 or 1913. A Danish immigrant, he had previously been a founding partner in two Midwestern pottery firms, the American Art Clay Works and Norse Pottery, both of Edgerton, Wisconsin.

At Bauer, Ipsen may have been the one responsible for modeling some of the fancy redware items produced at the time, such as the **Lion Pot,** the **Royal Pot,** the **Laurel Wreath Porch Pot,** and the very popular **Indian Bowl.** He certainly maintained a long and continuous association with the Bauer business, culminating in the company's greatest achievement: the introduction of **California Colored Pottery** around 1930.

Louis Ipsen

About the same time that Louis Ipsen arrived on the scene, another major Bauer player was relocating out west from his adopted home state of Arkansas. Matterson (Matt) Carlton arrived in Los Angeles with his family in 1915, working briefly at the Pacific Clay Products plant before joining forces with Andy Bauer and company. Carlton was already an accomplished turner when he started at Bauer and his talents were utilized to the fullest in the production of hand-thrown **Rebekah Vases, California Vases, Venus Vases, Rose Jars,** and **Carnation Vases.** The latter two were utilized by local florists to display long-stemmed roses, carnations, and other cut flowers.

The **Rebekah Vase** had been in production from an early date and was among the first items dipped in Bauer's newly developed matte green glazes. Since very early in the century, when the Grueby Pottery of Boston, Massachusetts, introduced its matte green art pottery to the public, demand for this type of ware had steadily risen. Along with the advent in the Southland of the Arts & Crafts Movement and the ubiquitous California bungalow style dwelling came increased local demand for the green glazed pots of numerous producers, including Bauer.

BAUER CHRONOLOGY

1885
Paducah Pottery is organized in Paducah, Kentucky, by John (Andy) Bauer.

1909
Construction begins on new Los Angeles, California, facility.

1910
J. A. Bauer Pottery is established in Los Angeles by Andy Bauer.

Production of red clay garden pottery and stoneware begins.

1911
Bauer family relocates to California from Kentucky.

1913
Louis Ipsen is hired as mold-maker, designer, and modeler.*

1915
Matt Carlton joins Bauer as turner/thrower.

1916
Bauer Pottery is awarded Bronze Medal at Panama-California Exposition in San Diego, California.

1919
First expansion of physical plant.

1922
Andy Bauer retires and sells two-thirds of business to Bernard Bernheim and one-third to daughter, Eva, and son-in-law, Watson E. Bockmon.

Ipsen is appointed superintendent of plant.*

Tracy Irwin joins Bauer as finisher.*

* = approximate date.

It is not known who formulated the matte green glazes at Bauer. It may have been the work of Ipsen. Whatever its source, the red clay wares that bore the low luster coating were prominently displayed in the J. A. Bauer Pottery Company exhibit at the Panama-California International Exposition held in San Diego during 1915–16. The firm's fleeting brush with art pottery did not go unrecognized. It received one of the two bronze medals given out at the fair in 1916. Even though this was not the coveted grand prize, it helped validate the effort, and certainly afforded Andy and his associates a moment of self-satisfaction.

Apparently the outbreak of the First World War had little negative effect on the pottery, since business seemed to expand and new markets opened up to the various articles the company turned out. Among these was a series of fancy new jardinieres with raised designs, including one with a Chinese-style dragon encircling its body. A **Mission Vase** was produced which was a loose adaption of the one made earlier by the Poxon China Company of Vernon (an industrial district southwest of downtown Los Angeles). Other intriguing red clay garden pots of the period included the **Jap Tub** and **Rustic Stump.**

Mission Vase

Success seemed to come easy for Andy Bauer and his Los Angeles firm; new products regularly found ready markets. A two-story addition to the existing facility had to be constructed in 1919, and many new workers were added to the payroll during this period just to keep pace with the growing popularity of the pottery. Much of the demand can be attributed to the unprecedented growth the Southland was just beginning to experience. During the next decade the population would more than double as more and more Easterners and Midwesterners flocked to the sunny land of opportunity.

In 1922, partly because he had reached retirement age and partly the result of failing health, John Andrew Bauer decided it was time to retire. Prosperity had allowed him to build a sprawling bungalow-style estate for himself and his wife in South Pasadena, invest in ranch land southeast of Los Angeles, and provide a comfortable home for each of his five children. By any measure an abundance of good fortune was his despite a lingering asthmatic condition he had been unable to whip. But it was not his destiny to enjoy a lengthy retirement as he died less than a year later.

A third of the pottery that Andy Bauer had directed so successfully from its inception in 1909, was sold to his daughter, Eva, and her husband Watson E. (Wat) Bockmon. The other two-thirds was purchased by Kentucky whiskey baron, Bernard Bernheim, who turned it over to his two sons, Sam and Lynn. The Bernheim brothers, who were heirs to their father's whiskey fortune, had no knowledge of running a pottery business. Also essentially unskilled was Wat, who had been a traveling salesman prior to his active involvement in the family business.

Bockmon was named president of the new partnership, probably because he had some marketing experience and was family. Lynn, the more assertive of the two brothers, became vice-president, while Sam was named secretary-treasurer. It was an unlikely arrangement that soon enough turned antagonistic. Wat and Lynn disagreed on most everything, especially when it came to financial matters. Wat was rather frugal while Lynn liked nothing better than to spend money on new equipment or whatever else he thought was necessary to improve the business. By 1928, the partnership had become untenable for Bockmon, and he withdrew.

Left to their own devices, the Bernheims proceeded to run things their own peculiar way. Lynn insisted on strict operating hours, which meant no waiting on drive-in customers before or after closing time. Unfortunately, many disgruntled customers found that nearby Pacific Clay Products was more than willing to satisfy their needs. The Bernheims' eagerness to make capital improvements did result in the erection of a fireproof storage shed for the firm's master molds, which proved to be a lifesaver when a fire occurred midway into the next decade.

Plant One, circa 1920.

Covered crocks bolstered the business at just the right time, thanks to the government ban on alcoholic beverages known as Prohibition. Beer (or home-brew) crocks, in sizes ranging from one-half gallon to twenty gallons, became big sellers, along with white and brown glazed whiskey jugs (available in five gallon capacities). Near the end of the decade, modeler Ipsen added a short set of heavy, rather crude dishes, to the subcategory of stoneware known as yellow ware. These dishes joined already popular pitcher and mug set (both jiggered and hand-thrown styles), ramekins, custard cups, spice jars, marmalade jars, and nested sets of mixing bowls and pudding dishes.

Probably the most auspicious act of the Bernheim tenure at Bauer was the hiring in 1929 of University of Illinois-trained ceramic engineer, Victor F. Houser. Arriving in California the previous year, Houser had been employed briefly at the Whittier Terra Cotta works before learning of the Bernheims' need for someone with ability in glaze chemistry. One of Houser's first actions after joining Bauer was to put a few of his opaque colored glazes to the test on Ipsen's new dishes. Previous to this the high-glaze colors used on Bauer pottery were basically two: a somewhat thin (transparent) dark green and cobalt blue. But why the desire for a new set of colors? Although this question may be unanswerable, perhaps management was seeking something to boost sales as the beer crock business began to slack off. Maybe they had gotten wind of developments on Santa Catalina Island (where Catalina Clay Products was generating some colorful art and garden pottery). For whatever reason, the introduction of Houser's brilliant new colors on Ipsen's dishes proved a momentous event.

To fully appreciate the revolutionary nature of this development, one need only examine the limited options available for setting a table prior to 1930. Most dinnerware in stores (not only in California, but throughout the country) was fragile, white-bodied earthenware or china decorated with delicate, sometimes fussily painted patterns (or similar decals). American-made versions of traditional European designs were generally the most affordable option. As Houser dipped Ipsen's simple, robust stoneware into his bright

1923
Andy Bauer dies.

1926
W. E. Bockmon's nephew, Jim Bockmon, joins firm as salesman.*

1927
W.E. Bockmon temporarily withdraws and establishes tile business in east Los Angeles.

Bernheim sons, Lynn and Sam, operate pottery.

Fireproof storage for master molds is constructed.

Ipsen creates short set of stoneware dishes.*

1929
Victor Houser is hired as chief ceramic engineer; develops new series of opaque colored glazes.

W. E. Bockmon buys out Bernheims and becomes president of firm.

1930
Ipsen's "plain" dinnerware is introduced in Houser's colored glazes.

1933
Ipsen adds ruffled/ring designs to dinnerware and kitchenware. Combination of "ring" and "plain" ware become **California Colored Pottery.**

New periodic kilns are added to plant.

Fred Johnson is hired as turner/thrower.

John Herbert (Herb) Brutsche joins business; begins as glazer, then becomes salesman.

* = approximate date.

opaque colored glazes, an all-new *American* dinnerware tradition was born! When it came time to market the new dishes, Bauer's salesmen turned to the nurseries that had been the company's main customers for its flower pots and other garden wares.

Although the concept of indoor-outdoor dining was not new to residents of Southern California, with their year-round sunshine and enclosed patios, a table service specifically suited to this task was. Bauer lead the way in 1930 with its unveiling of **California Colored Pottery.** Coinciding with these colorful events was another shake-up in management. Watson Bockmon was back, after an unsuccessful attempt to manufacture and sell floor tile, with a "deal" for the Bernheims. Apparently it was one they couldn't refuse, because the end result was a Bockmon buy-out and installation of himself as president once again. This time there would be no interference from unwanted partners with Wat in sole command of the situation. But the situation had changed dramatically since his stormy departure. Color was now the rage at Bauer! More new colors from Houser's palette were finding their way onto more and more new shapes in dinnerware, kitchenware, and even flower pots.

Ring beer pitcher and matching mugs.

At first, Bockmon was not too keen on the idea of colored pottery, but when he realized that it would be his company's salvation during the hard times of the Depression he quickly changed his tune. The simple "plain" ware which introduced the earliest colors (Chinese yellow, jade green, delph blue) was joined in 1933 by a full complement of ruffled or "ring" dishes and accessories. By then more of the familiar colors — orange red, royal blue, and black — had been added. Other colors were tried out on garden ware and later added to the dinnerware/kitchenware line. The throw rings encircling a garden pot that modeler Harold Johnson had created a few years earlier, may have been the stimulus for the embellishment of rings on Ipsen's dishes.

As colored pottery caught on with the buying public it became clear to Bauer's competitors (who were by now reeling from the effects of the stock market crash) that color was it. Soon neighboring Pacific Clay was producing a strong (though derivative) line called Hostessware. Before long other Los Angeles shops, including Metlox, Gladding-McBean, Vernon Kilns, and Meyers, had jumped on the colored pottery bandwagon. Catalina Clay Products may have been the earliest to market their own colorful line of dishes, but were largely unnoticed on the California mainland owing to the island's relative isolation.

One local company that failed to heed the warning signs of the Depression was Batchelder-Wilson. Widely known for his distinctive architectural tile, Ernest A. Batchelder refused to believe that the slow-down in Southern California's construction boom would be a long one. When bankruptcy finally came, Watson Bockmon wisely purchased the neighboring facility on Artesian Street. With the addition of a large and technically sophisticated plant (which became known as Bauer's Plant Two), production of numerous new lines soon commenced. One of the first was the tableware line known as **Monterey.** Half of this pattern was fashioned by Louis Ipsen and the other half was designed and modeled by a newcomer to Bauer, Ray Murray.

While Ipsen modeled the rudimentary pieces like plates, cups, and bowls, and the original round accessories, Murray, who had previously worked for Frankoma Pottery (in Oklahoma), added the "oval" (actually rectangular) shaped items to the line and one of its most striking and elusive pieces, the refrigerator beverage dispenser.

Fred Johnson and Ray Murray

New ware required new glaze colors. Victor Houser obliged with an array consisting of Monterey blue, turquoise blue, California orange-red (slightly darker than the original), canary yellow, burgundy, green, red brown, and white. A special clay body was formulated by Houser for Plant Two which contained talc and was semi-vitreous. Another new line, **High-Fire,** was added in honor of this new body. Introduced about the same time as **Monterey,** it consisted of jiggered "ring"-like kitchen accessories (mixing bowls, pie plates, etc.), garden pots, and hand-thrown floral containers by Fred Johnson. Johnson, who was Matt Carlton's nephew, joined the business in 1934. Before leaving his native Arkansas, he had been a principal thrower for Niloak Pottery in Benton.

Carlton was kept busy at Plant One throwing a wide assortment of vessel forms on the wheel. Since most of the handmade dishes that were originally included in the **California Colored Pottery** package were discontinued soon after the "ring" additions, Carlton was free to concentrate on his distinctive handmade vases, flower pots, candleholders, and so on. These were produced exclusively at Plant One in the same colored glazes as the "ring" dinnerware. Additional Houser colors used at Plant One included ivory, dusty burgundy, and white. Carlton's artware and the other colored pottery was bisque-fired in the old periodic kilns along with the rest of the stoneware. A second glost (glaze) firing was performed in the "beehive" kilns with the same items nestled among the red clay pots. This meant that Houser's lead-based glazes had to withstand the billowing gases produced by impurities inherent in the red clay. In September of 1935, a disruptive fire struck Plant One. This event was one that most large potteries had to endure. Fortunately, the Bernheims' fire-proof addition to the plant spared the master molds and production was halted for only a short time.

La Linda, another new Plant Two entry, was introduced to the public around 1938. It was the second Ipsen creation augmented

1935

Fire occurs, but master molds are spared.

W. E. Bockmon purchases nearby Batchelder-Wilson factory, and it becomes Bauer's Plant Two.

Bauer employees Paul Cauldwell and C. J. Malone leave to found Cemar Potteries in Los Angeles.

Houser formulates new talc body for use at Plant Two.

1936

Ispen's **Monterey** is first line produced at Plant Two.

1937

Plant Two's **Hi-Fire** line is created; includes Fred Johnson's hand-thrown items.

Ray Murray is hired; works at Plant Two as designer, modeler, and mold maker.

James (Jim) Johnson is hired; assists father, Fred Johnson.

1938

Murray adds additional items to **Monterey** line.

Cal-Art line, designed by Murray, is produced at Plant Two.

W. E. Bockmon purchases winery in Atlanta, Georgia, and converts it into Bauer satellite factory.

1940

Most "plain" ware in **California Pottery** line is phased out.

to be unadorned. Plates had smooth contours and a wide rim. Whereas **Monterey's** rim contained a graduated set of grooved rings, **La Linda's** were blank. The line debuted in a series of silky satin-matte pastel colors, but disappointing sales led to Houser's reformulation of the colors in high-gloss in the early forties. By this time the government restriction on use of certain metals (a result of our involvement in World War II) was beginning to wreck havoc with the ceramic industry. Houser was forced to create the new glazes without lead and without the standard opacifier, tin. Although he characterized them as "pretty crummy," they proved very popular. **La Linda** tableware became a wartime bestseller.

A line of kitchenware with the non-glamorous moniker, **Gloss Pastel Kitchenware (GPK),** was

Aladdin teapot

marketed about the time that **La Linda** got its facelift of new glazes. Designed entirely by Ray Murray, the new line consisted of many of the same kitchen articles found in the "ring" line but the rings this time were much wider, with a subtle increase in width from bottom to top. Mixing bowls, casseroles, pitchers, and cookie jars were made in green, yellow, light blue, dark blue, ivory, pink, and brown —many of the same colors used on the "new" **La Linda**. Unquestionably the highlight of the **GPK** line (and one of Bauer's classics) was a teapot known to collectors as the **Aladdin.**

Before our nation's entry into the Second World War, Watson Bockmon came up with a grand plan to expand his pottery empire. The Los Angeles business had been good to Wat and Eva Bockmon, and since they were now the sole proprietors, they were also the main beneficiaries of its success. Up to this point their plant had focused its sales outreach on states west of the Rocky Mountains. But Mr. Bockmon must have desired a piece of the action on the other side of this great divide. And being from Tennessee, he looked to the South for a strategic location from which to conquer the Eastern market. What he found was an abandoned winery in Atlanta, Georgia. Since the property was a bargain, it only added to the urgency to purchase it. In 1938, a contingent from the Los Angeles plant was dispatched to Atlanta to overhaul the place and outfit it properly for ceramic production. Bernard Jackson, a loyal company man, was given the task of administering the transformation, while Houser was called on to formulate new clay bodies and glazes.

Unfortunately, Watson E. Bockmon collapsed and died as the Bauer Pottery of Atlanta was just getting underway. John Herbert Brutsche, another Bauer colleague, took over management of the new operation, while Wat's nephew James (Jim) Bockmon became the Los Angeles plant's general manager. As war loomed ever closer, Brutsche bid on defense contracts and was awarded the task of manufac-

W. E. "Wat" Bockmon

Plant Two crew, 1938

turing two essential items for the U.S. Navy: hotel-grade china cereal bowls and tumblers. This was all the Atlanta plant produced for the duration of the war. In Los Angeles an increased production of stoneware poultry feeders and fonts (chicken became an essential food for the troops) forestalled the loss of key personnel to the war effort.

In 1945, with the global conflict concluded, Bauer-Atlanta set about preparing for its greatest challenge: the production of a line of floral artware designed by noted industrial designer Russel Wright. Really only a stopgap measure before Brutsche's planned conversion of the business to sanitary ware, a line by Wright could have been prestigious for the business. Instead, the project turned out to be a nightmare. Technical problems arose at every turn. The individual pieces, twenty designs in all, were unusually heavy, and Wright's custom-designed glazes often ran off the sides and stuck to the fireclay slabs. Explosions in the kiln also caused problems and setbacks. To add insult to injury, repeat orders were not forthcoming when the line finally reached the market. Russel Wright's vision was either too advanced or too bizarre for the public's taste at the time. Today, it has become the ultimate Bauer collectible!

Herb Brutsche remained in Atlanta until 1947 to convert Bauer-Atlanta into sanitary ware production under the name Georgia Sanitary Pottery. The company, after a deal was worked out with Peerless (another manufacturer of sanitary products whose Indiana plant had recently burned to the ground), launched the successful "Dixie" line of toilets and lavatories which continued in production until the late seventies. When Brutsche returned to Los Angeles with big plans for modernization and revision of the parent establishment, he was greeted with little enthusiasm. Although he was president of the Atlanta pottery and had become (along with wife, Virginia) half owner of the Los Angeles factory, he could not convince Jim Bockmon and others in management to install automated equipment and develop a contemporary line to replace the old and slumping (sales-wise) "ring" dinnerware. So like his father-in-law before him, Brutsche withdrew and established an entirely separate business.

Herb Brutsche

Brusché (the "t" was dropped) Ceramics was established in 1948 in Whittier. Because it was located on property owned by image-conscious Rose Hills Memorial Park, the fledgling operation was forced to relocate to Glendale a couple of years later. The company's **Al Fresco** dinnerware was inspired in part by Russel Wright's innovative and highly successful American Modern

1941
Murray's **Gloss Pastel Kitchenware** is produced at Plant Two in new Houser glazes.

Houser's gloss pastel glazes are added to **La Linda** line.

Herb Brutsche obtains defense contract. Bauer-Atlanta produces bowls and tumblers for the Navy.

1942
Wartime restriction is placed on essential metals used in glaze formulas.

Houser becomes supervisor of Plant Two.

Bauer-Los Angeles produces additional poultry feeders and fonts for war effort.

1943
Monterey line is discontinued.*

Uranium use is restricted by government. Orange-red glazes are gradually phased out.

Incursion by Brotherhood of Operating Potters at Bauer-Los Angeles.

1946
Bauer-Atlanta introduces short-lived artware line designed by **Russel Wright.**

Mary Wright designs **Country Gardens** tableware, but only prototypes are produced.

Louis Ipsen dies; Matt Carlton retires.

1947
Bauer-Atlanta plant is converted to Georgia Sanitary Pottery.

Brutsche returns to Los Angeles.

* = approximate date

line. Tracy Irwin modeled most of the shapes after Herb Brutsche's rough sketches, while Victor Houser provided the glaze formulas.

Al Fresco got a big boost from the Museum of Modern Art when it was featured in its Good Design exhibition at the Chicago Merchandise Mart in 1950. Nevertheless, the disrupting move to Glendale ultimately forced Brutsche to arrange for Bauer to continue production of his promising creation.

By this time, Jim Bockmon had come to the realization that an up-to-date dinnerware design was needed by the company and had already assigned the task to Tracy Irwin. Based on Irwin's previous work for Brusché Ceramics, and an acute awareness of the success of Wright's American Modern, **Monterey Moderne** was introduced just prior to **Al Fresco's** consolidation with Bauer. The two lines were very similar and were produced in many of the same glossy glazes: pink, yellow, chartreuse, olive green, brown, gray, burgundy, and black. They were both coupe designs: rimless and ringless. Basically these were no nonsense, form-follows-function dishes, anticipating one of the dominant dinnerware trends of the fifties.

As Bauer hit the mid-century mark, the company faced increased competition from the legion of local potteries that had made inroads during World War II — the heyday of Southern California's ceramic industry. One of these firms, Cemar, could be considered a Bauer spin-off, as it was the brainchild of two of their employees, Paul Cauldwell and C. J. Malone. Founded in the mid-thirties, Cemar produced decorative florist ware, figurines, and kitchenware, and it gave Bauer some serious competition with its florist line and kitchenware. When the company failed in the mid-fifties, Jim Bockmon bought the master molds and put many of its current items into production at Plant One.

Cemar cookie jar

By this time serious losses of key personnel had occurred or were just about to at the two Los Angeles plants. A brief rundown of these events would include Ray Murray's departure in 1941, Louis Ipsen's death and Matt Carlton's retirement in 1946, Fred Johnson's retirement in 1950, and Victor Houser's departure in 1951. The most catastrophic, however, was the sudden death in 1955 of general manager, Jim Bockmon, at age 51. He had been the company's guiding light from the time of his uncle's own sudden passing in 1939. With no immediate family she could call on to take over, Eva Bockmon appointed Bernard Jackson to fill the vacant post. Jackson, who had been around longer than most Bauer employees, got the nod for loyalty rather than for his managerial skills. After a rather lackluster stint as manager, he retired in 1960.

Misfortune beset the J. A. Bauer Pottery Company in the waning years of the 1950s: the loss of many skilled workers, irresolute management, increased competition from local manufacturers, low-cost Japanese imports, the widespread acceptance of cheaper plastics, and last but not least, mounting labor unrest. The incursion by the Brotherhood of Operating Potters that

1948
Brusché Ceramics is established in Whittier, California.

Al Fresco dinnerware is introduced.

1949
Tracy Irwin's **Monterey Moderne** dinnerware is produced at Bauer.

1950
Al Fresco is included in Museum of Modern Art's "Good Design" exhibit at Chicago Merchandise Mart.

Brusché **Al Fresco** is added to Bauer line.

Fred Johnson retires.

1951
Victor Houser departs and Jim Johnson takes over as glaze chemist and supervisor of Plant Two.

1953
Irwin's **Mission Moderne** line is created.*

* = approximate date

occurred in the early forties (in response to charges of low wages) had fostered a climate of tension between workers and management. This labor unrest was probably the greatest single challenge facing John Herbert Brutsche as he reluctantly assumed the post of general manager after Jackson's exit.

One of Brutsche's first actions, in an attempt to streamline production, was the installation of a ram press. This machine, which automatically stamps out ware from thin slabs of clay, was used to manufacture a new oven-serve line called **Moonsong**. Comprised of fifteen related items, **Moonsong** was introduced in early 1961 in speckled satin-matte glazes formulated by Jim Johnson. Jim, who was Fred Johnson's son, had joined the firm in 1937 to assist his father at the wheel (by finishing the pieces and later throwing some of the same forms). At the time of Houser's departure, Jim Johnson was assisting him in the supervision of Plant Two and in glaze chemistry. Afterwards he took the helm in both these capacities, and was the one responsible for the new glazes added in the fifties.

Jim Johnson

Brusché's **Al Fresco** was given a more singular identity in 1961 with the addition of satin-finish colors: Indio brown, pumpkin, spicy green, slate, desert beige, and champagne white. The new packaging was dubbed **Contempo**. The last new tableware produced by Bauer was a short set (unnamed) designed by Tracy Irwin and introduced the same year as **Al Fresco**. This too was produced in speckled satin-matte glazes and formally resembled some of the floral artware Irwin had created for the business during the fifties.

By 1961, the end was near. In October of that year the union members approved a general strike and picket lines went up at entrances to both plants. Very little work continued after that. Eva Bockmon, who had the final word, shared her late husband's parsimony (she even surpassed him in this regard), and adamantly refused to give in to the union's demand for a fair wage settlement. The operation was shut down in March of 1962. Sadly, the J. A. Bauer Pottery, a Los Angeles institution for more than fifty years, ceased to exist.

1955
Cemar molds are purchased and many items are added to Bauer line in Johnson's speckled glazes.

Jim Bockmon dies. Bernard Jackson appointed as general manager by Eva Bockmon.

Tracy Irwin designs numerous new additions to Bauer's floral artware line.

1960
Bernard Jackson retires; Herb Brutsche assumes post of general manager.

1961
Brutsche installs ram press.

Moonsong oven-serve line is produced in Johnson's matte glazes.

New glazes transform **Al Fresco** line into "new" Brusché **Contempo** dinnerware.

Unnamed line (#300) of dishes and kitchenware is fashioned by Irwin.

General strike is called.

1962
Eva Bockmon refuses to bend to union demands. J. A. Bauer Pottery is closed.

ART POTTERY

I confess to having a problem with the term "art pottery." Are all other kinds of pottery not to be considered art? I understand what is intended by the appellation but still have trouble whenever I encounter it. With that said, an examination of Bauer's art pottery endeavor can be attempted without rancor.

Around the time Matt Carlton joined the business in 1915, Andy Bauer and associates were either contemplating or experimenting with an art line that would eventually include vases, low bowls, flower frogs, jardinieres, flower pots, flower pot saucers, ashtrays, and bookends. Though some of these items were slip cast, the bulk of them were thrown individually on the potter's wheel. Vases and other floral containers more than sustained the effort. Specific forms were given names: Rebekah and California vases (ranging from 8" to 24" in height), Venus vases (6" to 16"), rose jars (5" to 24", in two circumference groups), and carnation jars (6" to 24"). The rose and carnation jars were used primarily by florists to display cut flowers.

The cast ware included jardinieres and flower pots in both plain and ornamented designs. At least two cast vases were produced: the 9" Mission vase and a bud vase/candleholder made in 6" and 8" heights. The popular Indian bowls were offered in a variety of sizes and proved ideal accouterments for the ubiquitous California bungalow. Bauer's version of the regulation matte green glaze, so prevalent during the Craftsman period, involved two very different outcomes. The more interesting of the two types (#1) was a satin-matte green containing scattered iridescent patches and/or darkened (almost black) specks. The other (#2) was a thoroughly dead mossy green with a somewhat craggy texture. Both glazes were applied over Bauer's standard redware body, which was also used to make common red clay flower pots.

The company exhibited its art pottery at an international exposition organized in celebration of the newly completed Panama Canal which

Left to right: 9" California vase, glaze #2, $500.00; 10" rose jar, glaze #1, $750.00+; 5½" vase (or ewer), glaze #2, $300.00; 10" Venus vase, glaze #2, $400.00; 9" vase, glaze #2, $500.00.

took place in San Diego's Balboa Park during 1915–16. The awards jury bestowed one of two Bronze Medals given out in 1916 to the J. A. Bauer Pottery for its artware display. Although not a first place award, it nevertheless provided encouragement for the upstart business. Despite the accolade, green glazed art pottery was phased out almost entirely by the mid-twenties.

Only one consistently marked example of Bauer's brief foray into art pottery has been observed: the 3" x 6" (small circumference) Rose jar — possibly a salesman's sample (see marks below). Most other pieces, even cast items, will be found without identifying marks. A few interesting color variations have been noted. For instance the #2 matte green was occasionally enhanced by a dark green dripped over the lighter undercoating. A cobalt blue matte-glazed low bowl is shown in one of the color plates. This highly unusual variation adds considerable value to an otherwise typical form. Examples of the #2 matte green with glaze crawling on the surface must be considered as seconds.

*Pair of very rare bookends with raised California bear motif, glaze #2,
$2,000.00+; 8" vase with dark green overdrip (rare), $950.00+.*

*Left to right: 10" low flower bowl with dark green overdrip (rare), $900.00+; 12" low flower bowl
in very rare matte cobalt blue glaze, $1,000.00+.*

Flower holder, 2" x 4½", glaze #1, $85.00.   *6" jardiniere, glaze #2, $400.00+.*

Left to right:
Top row: 15" Rebekah vase, glaze #1, $1,500.00+; 8" Rebekah vase, glaze #2, $750.00; 10"
Rebekah vase, glaze #2, $950.00.
Center row: 10" low flower bowl, glaze #2, $200.00; 5" vase, glaze #2, $300.00; 8" vase with
dark green overdrip (rare), $950.00+; 6" Venus vase, glaze #1, $300.00+.
Bottom row: 9" jardiniere, glaze #2, $400.00; 7" deep flower bowl, glaze #1, $275.00+, 8"
rose jar, glaze #1, $400.00+, 10" rose jar, glaze #2, $500.00.

Left to right: 10" jardiniere with raised filigree design, glaze #2, $750.00+; 12" Indian bowl, glaze #2, $2,000.00+. (Indian bowls are rare in matte green glazes.)

6" rose jar with mark, glaze #2, $250.00; 12" yellow ware tray, $50.00.

24" carnation jar, glaze #1, $1,800.00+; 24" Rebekah vase, glaze #2, $2,500.00+.

RED, WHITE & YELLOW WARE

The earliest Bauer goods were plain and fancy red clay flower pots, and many of them were still in production when the company closed. They constituted Bauer's bread & butter line — something the company could count on to keep things going. Cultivating gardens and potting plants were, and continue to be, popular recreation for many Californians, and Bauer was once the main supplier of common red clay pots for this activity.

The other type of ware produced in the very early years was whiteware, which was a white bodied stoneware. Much of the stoneware made during Bauer's first California decade was stock-in-trade transplanted from Paducah, Kentucky. Most of these items would be considered "primitives" today, and many are pictured in the early Bauer catalog reproduced in the Appendix.

Yellow ware, which was a yellow tinted stoneware, came into prominence in the twenties. Some of this "new" merchandise was originally produced as whiteware, but most items, like the handmade table and kitchen wares of the late twenties, were new additions to the line. Much of this yellow ware can also be observed in the above mentioned catalog.

Two of Bauer's most successful early garden pot designs. Left to right: 14" redware lion pot, $150.00. (Note: Lion pots continue to be reproduced and often, but not always, are glazed white.) 12" redware Indian bowl, $400.00. (Note: Indian bowls marked "American" may not be Bauer ware.)

Two of the most difficult to find redware garden items. Left to right: 12" rustic stump, $275.00+; 11" Jap tub, $175.00.

Mark on laurel wreath porch pot at right.

Left: 10" laurel wreath porch pot in redware, marked "J. A. Bauer Pottery Co. L.A. CAL/10," $200.00. Right: Redware pot that may often go unrecognized, the 9" x 6" rustic pan, $95.00.

Left: 12¾" (3 gallon) redware olla with faucet, $85.00. Center: (2 gallon) brown glazed fumigator, $100.00. Right: 17" (5 gallon) brown glazed jug, marked "Bauer Pottery Co. Los Angeles, Cal," $200.00.

Mark on redware olla with faucet.

Two Bauer churns, with the one at right likely dating somewhat earlier than the other. Left to right: 7" x 12¾" (2 gallon) whiteware churn, no cover, stamped mark on side, $100.00, with cover, $175.00; 2 gallon glazed redware churn, no cover, impressed mark on side, $95.00, with cover, $200.00.

Top row: Brown glazed 4-quart bean pot, marked "Bauer Pottery Co. Los Angeles, Cal,"
$65.00; 8-quart bean pot, marked "Bauer Pottery Co. Los Angeles, Cal," $135.00.
Bottom row: One-gallon glazed redware milk crock, $45.00.

Bauer whiteware, left to right: Two-piece 1-gallon sanitary chick font, marked "Bauer Los Angeles, Cal"
on underside of tray, $65.00; 1-lb. covered butter jar, hand decorated, marked "Bauer Los Angeles, Cal,"
$60.00; 10½" x 4½" (1-gallon) milk crock, $40.00.

Two small pin trays/ashtrays with raised Old West scene of Indian on horseback, possibly produced as gifts for valued employees or customers. Left to right: 4" tray, yellow ware, no inscription, $400.00+; 4" tray, cobalt blue, inscribed "J. A. Bauer Pottery Co. Los Angeles, Cal/Season Greetings 1929" on face, $500.00+.

A popular Bauer commodity during the home brew days of Prohibition: 17" (5 gallon) brown & white whiskey jug, stamped mark on side, $350.00+.

Rare 4½" cobalt glazed stoneware butter plate with inscription on bottom: "Merry Xmas/Happy New Year 1928/Bauer Pottery Co. Los Angeles, Cal," $350.00+.

Left to right: 4¾" whiteware jar, open, $25.00; 3¼" glazed redware condiment pot, open, marked "Bauer U.S.A.," $25.00; unusual 10½" whiteware jug without handles, stamped marked (upside down) on side, $95.00.

Below: Marks on jug and condiment pot.

Frog-shaped flower frog, 2" x 4½", cobalt blue glaze, $65.00.

Bauer's patented 5" ant trap, dark green, marked "Calpro Ant System Los Angeles, Cal" on top and "Pat. June 2, 1925" on bottom, $65.00.

Commonly called crocks, there were two distinct styles of whiteware covered jars — one without handles (more familiar, at left) and one made to be fitted with bail (wire and wood) handles. Left to right: 14½" h (6 gallon) jar, no cover, stamped mark on side, $175.00, with cover, $250.00; 15" h (8 gallon) jar, no cover or handles, stamped mark on side, $225.00, with cover and bail handle, $350.00+.

Early Bauer stoneware with a variety of glazes and decorative treatments.

Left to right:

Top row: 12" (3 quart) pitcher, handmade yellow ware, $500.00+; comparable pitcher, hand decorated (appealing decoration adds value to this example), $750.00+; 6¼" vase, swirl painted, $250.00; 6¼" vase, swirl painted, $250.00.

Center row: 3" mug, handmade yellow ware, $65.00+; 4" mug, handmade yellow ware, $75.00+; 3¾" mug, cobalt blue, $85.00+; 3¾" mug, dark green, $65.00+; 5" cream pitcher, handmade yellow ware, $200.00+; 5½" handmade cream pitcher, cobalt blue, $165.00+.

Bottom row: #12 (7¼") pitcher, rare blue mottled (spongeware) treatment, $275.00+; #30 (5¼") pitcher, hand-decorated yellow ware, $200.00; #30 pitcher, glazed redware, $100.00; #12 pitcher, yellow ware, $200.00.

Mark on bottom of #12 yellow ware pitcher in above photo.

Three handmade stoneware vases. Left to right: 10" California vase, very thin dark green, $395.00+; 10" Rebekah vase, dark green, $600.00+; 10½" Rebekah vase, polychrome spray painted, $500.00+.

10" cast jardiniere with raised dragon design, dark green, $350.00.

Left to right: Unusual 9½" lamp base, handmade yellow ware, $500.00+; #1 (4½") spice jar, yellow ware, $100.00; 4½" ashtray, cobalt blue, $60.00; 7" (3 quart) pitcher, handmade yellow ware, $500.00+.

The artistic side of Bauer's early stoneware production is in evidence here. Left to right: 4½" vase, $275.00; 8" bud vase/candlestick, $300.00; 9" Mission vase, $500.00+; 6" California vase, $275.00; 6" steamship vase, $250.00. (Note: All examples pictured are glazed inside only.)

An interesting decorative treatment for stoneware vases during the twenties consisted of a swirled polychrome painted effect, seen here on a variety of cast ware. Left to right: 6" California vase, $250.00; 6" carnation jar, $250.00; 7½" hyacinth jar, $200.00; 6½" vase, $250.00; 7" vase, solid black painted vase, $200.00; 6½" vase, $250.00; 7½" vase, $260.00.

Newly hired chemist Victor Houser utilized some of the bisque-finished artware stockpiled during the twenties to test his new opaque colors. The results (circa 1929–30), left to right: 9" Mission vase, jade green, $600.00+; 8" bud vase/candlestick, jade green, $450.00+; 8" rose jar, marked "Bauer Los Angeles," black, $800.00+; 7½" hyacinth jar, jade green, $500.00+. (Note: All examples are glazed cobalt blue inside.)

One of the most elusive Bauer cast stoneware vases of the twenties is this 5" peacock vase, bisque with dark green glaze inside, $600.00+.

6" low flower bowl, cobalt blue, $200.00; with matching duck-shaped flower frog, $65.00.

PLAIN WARE:
The Original California Colored Pottery

Sometime in the late twenties, designer Louis Ipsen got the bug to create a set of dishes for Bauer. The salesmen may have suggested it or management may have requested it. It may have seemed routine and inconsequential at the time, but now must be considered a momentous event. In retrospect, the creating of a short set of rather impromptu styled tableware for casual dining was just the start of what would ultimately lead to the company's greatest glory — **California Colored Pottery.**

Originally the dishes were issued in common yellow ware, a yellow tinted stoneware body with a transparent glaze. The first plates resembled flower pot liners. Most of the hollow ware forms (pitchers, mugs, sugar bowls, etc.) were hand-made by Matt Carlton, who possibly designed the shapes, making it a collaborative effort.

Conceptually, the new line was just the thing for outdoor dining, which was a developing proclivity in Southern California with its temperate climate and preference for informal living. By 1930, Ipsen's basic flatware had evolved into the simple vigorous style now familiar to collectors. When Victor Houser was hired in 1929 to create opaque colors for the company, he utilized the

greenware (unglazed pottery) to try-out his new glazes. The result did not go unnoticed. Soon the colorful results were displayed at nurseries and garden centers in and around Los Angeles.

The concept of mix 'n match was another new offering of the firm. The choice made available to consumers was pick a single colored set that matched throughout or mix the harmonious hues available at your own whim. A little fun was consequently added to the previously mundane task of selecting a table service. As more colors were added to the line, more buyer interest was aroused. It never takes long for a new trend to develop in Southern California, and one definitely was afoot in the Southland in the early years of the Depression.

By the time that the "ring" variation was added in 1933, the "plain" tableware included four different sized plates (including a 4½" butter plate), a coffee set (consisting of a one-quart pitcher, six four-ounce mugs, and a 10" round tray), a low and a tall handmade Dutch pitcher,

Victor F. Houser

a handmade sugar bowl and three sizes of cream pitcher, a cup and saucer, a six-cup teapot, a handmade "midget" sugar bowl and creamer, an eight-ounce baby mug, an individual coffee pot, two different sized grill (divided) plates, two different sized chop plates, an oval platter, a large salad bowl, a large wooden handled coffee server (with or without cover), along with ramekins and various sized mixing bowls, pudding dishes, and bean pots for food preparation.

The merging of the "plain" and "ring" styles offered up numerous new choices and may have presented a confusing aggregation to some potential customers. The entire assortment was dubbed **California Colored Pottery,** which was later shortened to **California Pottery.** Because of the instant popularity of "ring" ware and its overwhelming sales appeal, the "plain" items were gradually discontinued. By 1941, the only remaining "plain" items were the eight-ounce mug (formerly baby mug), the individual coffee pot, the smaller 10" grill plate, the ramekin, and the bean pots. Interesting late additions included a handmade Mexican hat ashtray and two sizes of square stacking ashtrays in metal stands, but the heart of the **California Pottery** line was "ring" ware. The "plain" had given way forever to the fancy.

Today, collectors continue to favor the "ring" line over its "plain" cousin. It may be just a situation where so little "plain' ware is available that collecting it is too difficult. Cups and saucers are especially scarce, as are handled soup bowls (cups having two handles). If you like it, then good luck in finding it!

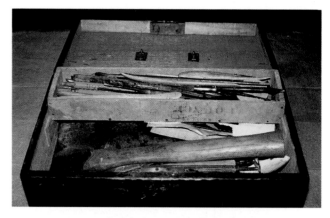

Louis Ipsen's toolbox.

Easy to find "plain" ramekins, $15.00–20.00; black, $30.00.

Dennis Ashlock, photo

Very rare large capacity "plain" mixing bowls. Left to right: #1, 3½ gallon, $500.00–800.00+ (black, $1,200.00+); #3, 2 gallon, $300.00–450.00+; #4, 1½ gallon, $200.00–300.00+; #6, 1¼ gallon, $150.00–225.00+ (black, $337.50+). Note: Late period yellow glaze on #3, $150.00; on #6, $75.00.

Chris Witzke, photo

Not exactly the coffee set pictured in Bauer catalogs of the thirties but close. 12" Dutch pitcher, $400.00–600.00+; 4½" mugs, $80.00–120.00 each; 14" tray, $125.00–175.00. Note: Pitcher and mugs are handmade by Matt Carlton.

A selection of handmade "plain" ware by Matt Carlton. Left to right:

Top row: 4½" lamp base, $300.00–450.00+; goblet (not handmade), $150.00–225.00+; midget sugar bowl, $125.00–175.00+; 5" pitcher, $150.00–225.00+; midget creamer, $65.00–95.00+.

Center row: Tumble-up set – 7" water bottle, $500.00+ with 2¾" tumbler, $30.00–45.00+; 4" individual bean pot, hand decorated, $125.00–175.00; 9" carafe, $350.00–525.00+.

Bottom row: 4" mug, $100.00–150.00; 12" pitcher, $400.00–600.00+; 4" mug, $100.00–150.00.

"Plain" ware service plates, front to back: 6½" bread & butter, $30.00–45.00 (black, $90.00+); 8½" salad, $65.00–95.00+; 9½" dinner, $65.00–95.00; 11½" dinner, $125.00–175.00+.

Typical in-mold mark of the 1930s.

Top row: Covered coffee server, $75.00–100.00 (cover only, $25.00–35.00); individual bean pot, $100.00–150.00; 3" square ashtray, $60.00–90.00+; metal holder for four ashtrays, $60.00+.

Bottom row: #6, 10¼" pudding dish, $80.00–120.00; #5, 9¼" pudding dish, $75.00–100.00; (black, $200.00+); #3, 7½" pudding dish, $50.00–75.00; #2, 6¼" pudding dish, $35.00–50.00; #1, 5¼" pudding dish, $30.00–45.00. (Note: missing #4, 8¼" pudding dish, $60.00–90.00.)

Top row: 4" handmade mug, $100.00–150.00; 3" handmade mug, $50.00–75.00; 2¾" tumbler, $30.00–45.00+; coffee cup, $150.00–225.00+; saucer, $25.00–35.00; beer mug, $250.00–375.00+; 8 oz. baby mug, $60.00–90.00.

Center row: 2-quart bean pot, $150.00–225.00; 8¼" salad bowl, $80.00–120.00; 10½" salad bowl, $100.00–150.00+.

Bottom row: Sugar bowl, $85.00–125.00+; creamer, $55.00–80.00; sherbet, $100.00–150.00+; 4½" butter plate, $50.00–75.00+ (black, $150.00+); individual bean pot, $100.00–150.00.

SO MANY RINGS...

What would Bauer be without its rings? Mitch Tuchman, author of *Bauer: Classic American Pottery*, has speculated that without the existence of the "ring" line, the overall status of Bauer Pottery as a collectible would be greatly diminished. And I certainly agree with him. It is primarily the "ring" dinnerware, kitchenware, and artware that collectors avidly seek today. I found during my many years as a dealer, that "ring" consistently out-sold all other Bauer ware. It continues to enjoy an exalted position in the collectible pottery pantheon, at least here in California. It was truly a phenomenon in its heyday, and its popularity among collectors has not abated.

Louis Ipsen's early "plain" dishes were simple and assured and had an undeniable charm, but around 1933, when he added overall rings to the profile of his pitchers and mugs, something electrifying resulted. The company, however, seemed at a loss to resolutely describe what Ipsen had created. In vintage catalogs the ware was termed "ring" and sometimes alternately "ruffle" or "ruffled." What was the problem? One of the key players in this drama, Victor Houser, relates that the rings may have been nothing more than an afterthought. An early flower pot design by Harold Johnson, who worked for Bauer very briefly around 1930, is credited with inspiring the added ridges. Whatever their source, the rings proved to be a sensation with the buying public. Gradually more and more new items were added to the line, which eventually became known simply as **California Pottery.** Originally the package included both "plain" and "ring/ruffle" shapes, in a kind of hodge-podge arrangement. Neither style constituted a complete set, nor were the two types very consistent or truly complementary.

Interestingly, the three raised ridges encircling the first "ring" pattern plates were decidedly subtle. If a production mold was overused, the result would be barely visible rings. Known among today's collectors as the "early period," these

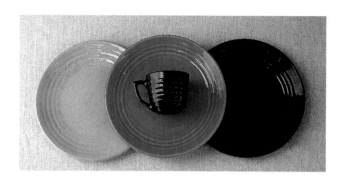

rather primitive dishes were probably not made very long — from 1933 to about 1936. All sizes of plates from the early period are usually found without identifying marks on the bottom. Many hollow ware pieces — pitchers, cups, tumblers — likewise were not marked. This lack of marking makes it especially difficult for the novice to distinguish the genuine article.

During the "middle period," roughly 1936 – 1946, flatware became more dish-like and the rings became more distinct. These and many other items in the line will be found consistently marked, generally with the circular imprinted "Bauer Los Angeles." The post-war "late period" flatware became even more hollowed out, having highly raised rings near the edge. For some unknown reason, these plates tended to be larger than before, as much as a half inch or more in diameter, depending on the type of plate. They were marked in-mold, as previously, except "Made In USA" was added to the center. A few hollow ware pieces also increased in size or capacity at this time, and some were streamlined, with elongated spouts on pitchers the most obvious enhancement.

It is not known precisely when the "ring" line was discontinued. It appears that most of the bestselling Bauer pattern was phased out in the late fifties. The only item remaining when the workers went on strike in 1961 was the nested set of mixing bowls. Changing trends and tastes coupled with the protracted production of the line undoubtedly contributed to its demise. But what a sensation the "ring" ware had created!

During its peak in the Southland, nothing out-sold it. As Brutsche said, "Every woman in Southern California knew Bauer." It initiated the mix 'n match trend in pottery tableware while it furnished the ideal service for the omnipresent patio. Coffee servers were especially popular for transferring everyone's favorite hot beverage from kitchen to patio. Matching tumblers with clip-on metal and wood handles completed the ensemble. Altogether more than 100 separate "ring" items were produced, with some enjoying longevity and others coming and going in the blink of an eye. Houser related that Ipsen and others were always "trying out new stuff" — coming up with prototypes for "ring" accessories just to see what the public reaction would be (or, what the wholesale buyers would accept).

Since some items were not appreciated by the buyers or public, the result was a very short production span which translates into rarity and generally big demand in today's market. Other accessories were deemed non-essential during the tough times of the Depression and were

Highly prized black and white "ring" ware. Clockwise from top: 8-cup coffee server with metal handle, $500.00+; sherbet, $300.00+; 5" bread & butter plate, $67.50+; goblet, $250.00+; coffee cup, $100.00+; saucer, $60.00+, 9" dinner plate, $200.00+; 7½" salad plate, $100.00+, 6" bread & butter plate, $80.00+; 4" berry bowl, $100.00+; salt, $60.00+; pepper, $50.00+. Note: All black/white prices are bottom line as all are hard to find.

passed up by the average consumer. Some of the more interesting "ring" items met with this fate, the prime example being the honey jar. These are extremely scarce these days and command huge sums when found!

Glaze color has become a major factor in evaluating Bauer Pottery, and nowhere is this more in evidence than in the "ring" line. For instance "ring" items in black, because of their scarcity, bring high prices these days. The black glaze's closest rival would be white and to some it ranks even higher on the current value scale. Yet neither of these colors was particularly popular during the years the line was produced. Over the years that I have been observing Bauer's progression, the status of certain standard colors has changed. For example, in the early days of collecting, and especially "ring" collecting, the orange-red glaze was hot while jade green generally got a cool reception. The tables have turned rather dramatically now, with green ranking higher than orange in overall acceptance among connoisseurs. (See "All About Pricing" chart for more details.)

According to Houser, Bauer's glaze chemist at the time, the earliest colors produced were Chinese yellow, delph blue, and jade green. These colors were tried out on a variety of ware, including examples of the bisque-finished stoneware that Ipsen had created in the early twenties. This trial period began in late 1929 or early 1930. Probably no new colors were added before 1931. Houser remembers that orange-red "came somewhat later."

It is very likely that royal (cobalt) blue was the fourth color produced, in 1931 or 1932, followed by orange-red, possibly as early as 1933. The orange color was made using depleted uranium oxide imported from Africa. Even though it was more expensive to manufacture this color, I have only been able to find one instance where the company charged more — in **Hi-Fire Pottery,** orange-red was 50% higher in price than the other colors.

White is an interesting study. I have never seen it listed in any company catalog or price list for the **California Pottery** line. I have come to believe that white was strictly a special order color, and possibly was added at the same time as black, around 1934. By 1939, a full spectrum of glaze colors had arrived on the scene, as ivory and burgundy were also listed in company literature. The standard colors became Chinese yellow, royal blue, orange-red, delph blue, jade green, black, ivory, and burgundy. The only addition to these colors prior to the fifties was light brown, which was made available only on a few selected items.

Some colors were only experimental and saw very limited production. They are considered simply curiosities in the current market. Among them are some of Houser's attempts to duplicate the orange-red glaze after uranium became an essential war material during World War II. What some collectors are calling "papaya," a bright yellow-orange, is probably just the **Contempo** pumpkin in gloss. After lead was requisitioned for the war effort, new lead-free substitutes were made for most of the standard colors. The new glazes were somewhat less opaque because tin, an opacifier, was yet another metal no longer available to the ceramics trade. Houser did his best to replicate the originals but definite differences are evident between old and new. Collectors tend to favor the older colored glazes, and I agree that they are aesthetically superior. On the other hand, they may pose a health threat to those who use their dishes on a regular basis.

The health question is one that periodically rears its ugly head. Probably no one can state conclusively that the lead-bearing early glazes used at Bauer are truly dangerous. If one is sensitive to lead, then obviously the dishes could pose a problem. My answer to anyone living in the Los Angeles area is simple: "Breathing the air is far more apt to kill you than eating off Bauer plates."

Rather than list the scarce or rare items in "ring" dinnerware/kitchenware, because these days so much of the line would come under one of these designations, I will attempt a rundown of the more commonly found pieces. Included would be 9" dinner plates, 6" bread & butter plates, 6" saucers, 4" berry bowls, custard cups, 9" low salad bowls, beating bowls, 2-quart batter bowls, 10" oval vegetable bowls, all sizes/types of coffee servers, creamers, sugar bowls, 12" chop plates 12" oval platters, most salt and pepper shakers, 6-ounce tumblers, smaller sizes of the standard pitcher, most sizes of the casserole (not the individual casserole), smaller sized mixing bowls (#36 is somewhat scarce), and the "scallop" design pickle dish. All of the above listed items will not be readily found in the less common glaze colors (burgundy, ivory, black, etc.), and the scarcity factor will vary from one locale to another. This list is based solely on my personal experience shopping the California market.

Elusive "ring" footed salad/punch bowls. Left to right: 14" punch bowl, $1,000.00+; 9" salad/punch bowl, $500.00+; 11" salad/punch bowl, $750.00+.

Top row: 6-cup teapot, $250.00–375.00 (black, $750.00+); barrel-shaped mug, $300.00–450.00+; barrel-shaped tumbler with metal handle, $150.00–225.00+; beer mug, $300.00–450.00+; beer pitcher, $1,000.00+.

Center row: Divided oval vegetable bowl, $250.00–375.00+; 8" oval vegetable bowl, $125.00–175.00; 10" oval vegetable bowl, $125.00–175.00.

Bottom row: 9" oval platter, $75.00–100.00; gravy bowl, $200.00–300.00; 12" oval platter, $60.00–90.00.

Top row: #18 mixing bowl, $85.00–125.00; #24 mixing bowl, $75.00–100.00 (black, $200.00+); #30 mixing bowl, $50.00–75.00; rare copper-plated metal caddy and ice tongs, $200.00+; #36 mixing bowl, $50.00–75.00.

Center row: #9 mixing bowl, $150.00–225.00; #12 mixing bowl, $100.00–150.00 (Note: All above mixing bowls have three inside rings); restyled creamer, $50.00–75.00; sugar bowl, $75.00–100.00; 2½" candleholder, $75.00–100.00; creamer, $40.00–60.00.

Bottom row: #9 nappy, $150.00–225.00; #8 nappy, $125.00–175.00; #7 nappy, $100.00–150.00; #6 nappy, $85.00–125.00; #5 nappy, $50.00–75.00.

Top row: Cookie jar, $750.00+; #1 spice jar, $200.00–300.00+; #2 spice jar, $300.00–450.00+; #3 spice jar, $500.00+.

Center row: Drip coffee pot, $1,500.00+; 2-cup teapot, $125.00–175.00; A.D. cup, $125.00–175.00+; A.D. saucer, $65.00–95.00+; 6-cup teapot with wood handle, $300.00–450.00+.

Bottom row: Soufflé or ice bowl, $500.00+ (not shown: very rare cover $500.00+); 2-quart batter bowl, $150.00–225.00; 1-quart batter bowl, $300.00–450.00.

Right: View of "ring" spice jar showing cover.

A rainbow of "ring" plates. Front to back: 5" bread & butter, $60.00–90.00+; 6" bread & butter, $20.00–30.00; 7½" salad, $35.00–50.00; 9" dinner, $30.00–45.00; 10½" dinner, $100.00–150.00+.

The very evasive "ring" cigarette jar, $750.00+.

"Ring" low salad bowls. Left to right: 9" size, $75.00–100.00; 12" size, $125.00–175.00; 14" size, $250.00–375.00+.

"Ring" bowls for festive or casual meals. Left to right: 7½" soup plate, $80.00–120.00+; 4" berry bowl, $45.00–65.00; 4½" cereal bowl, $55.00–85.00; 5" fruit bowl, $50.00–75.00.

Thirst-quenching helpers in the "ring" line. Left to right: 12 oz. tumbler, $60.00–90.00; handle, $15.00–20.00; 6 oz. tumbler, white, $100.00+; 6 oz. tumbler, $30.00–45.00; handle, $10.00–15.00; water bottle, open, $125.00–175.00; rare cover, $750.00+; goblet, $125.00–175.00 (black, $350.00+); 3 oz. tumbler, $85.00–125.00+; unusual handled 3 oz. tumber, $150.00–225.00+.

The "ring" butter dishes. Left to right: ¼-lb. oblong design, $250.00–375.00; round design, $250.00–375.00.

Irving Scible, photo

In back: "Ring" relish plate, $85.00–125.00. Left: Hi-Fire "ring" ashtray/nut cups, $25.00–35.00 each; in holder, $75.00–100.00. Right: Very elusive "ring" mustard jar, $750.00+.

Very rare cover for regular size "ring" creamer, jade green, $300.00+.

All sizes of Bauer's standard "ring" pitcher design. Left to right: 3 qt. size, $250.00–375.00; 2 qt. size, $150.00–225.00; 1 qt. size, $100.00–150.00; 1½ pint size, $55.00–80.00; creamer, $40.00–60.00.

The evolution of the "ring" sugar bowl. Left: Early design, very rare, $250.00–375.00+. Center: Standard design, $75.00–100.00. Right: Larger, late period model, $75.00–100.00.

Top row: 8-cup covered coffee server with wood handle, $125.00–175.00 (marked "San Diego Expo," $250.00–375.00+); 6-cup open coffee server with wood handle, $75.00–100.00; 8-cup coffee server with metal handle, $100.00–150.00 (white, $500.00+).

Center row: Cream (syrup) pitcher, $300.00–450.00; beating bowl, $75.00–100.00, beating bowl pitcher, $200.00–300.00; very rare cover for beating bowl pitcher, $500.00+.

Bottom row: 2 qt. pitcher, $150.00–225.00; restyled pitcher, $200.00–300.00; ball pitcher, $350.00–525.00+.

Mark sometimes found on 8-cup coffee servers.

Top row: 6" vase, $300.00–450.00+; 5" bud vase, $200.00–300.00+; sherbet, $85.00–125.00+; 14" pedestal bowl, $750.00+.

Center row: Jumbo cup, $100.00–150.00+; A.D. cup & saucer, $200.00–300.00+; coffee cup, $65.00–95.00 (black, $150.00+); tea or punch cup, $45.00–65.00; coffee/tea saucer, $25.00–35.00.

Bottom row: 8½" casserole, $200.00–300.00; 2" ashtray, $65.00–95.00+; 7½" casserole, $150.00–225.00; 6½" casserole, $125.00–175.00; casserole frame (all sizes, except individual), $40.00–60.00.

Left: Very hard-to-find 5½″ "ring" individual casserole, $300.00–450.00+. Right: "Ring" refrigerator jar, $60.00–90.00; cover, $60.00–90.00; frame, $60.00–90.00.

The "ring" refrigerator jars, shown at right, make leftovers more appealing. Set as pictured, $375.00.

Kitchen helpers in "ring" line. Left to right: 2 qt. batter bowl, $150.00–225.00; less common 1 qt. batter bowl, $300.00–450.00+.

Chop plates in the "ring" line. Left to right: 17" size, $250.00–375.00+; 14" size, $100.00–150.00; 12" size, $75.00–100.00.

Do not confuse the common 4" covered baking dish, left, $45.00–65.00, with the very elusive 5½" lug soup bowl, $150.00–225.00+, and cover, $200.00–300.00+.

Two of the most coveted "ring" items. Left to right: Sugar shaker, $500.00+; egg cup, $300.00–450.00+.

These small round "ring" ashtrays are very hard to find. Left to right: 2″ size, $65.00–95.00+; 4″ model, $100.00–150.00+. Not shown: Similar 5½″ ashtray, $150.00–225.00.

In-mold recessed mark found on third period "ring" items. Same mark without the "Made in USA" can be found on second period ware.

Not many collectors can boast ownership of the very rare "ring" honey jar in either of its manifestations, single bee cover or double bee cover. Honey jar, open, $500.00+; cover (both styles), $1,000.00+; complete jar, $3,000.00+.

This ice water pitcher, often mistaken for Monterey, was listed in Bauer's California Pottery catalog as number 58. It may have been designed at the same time the Monterey line was being developed. Shown here in jade green, $300.00–450.00+.

MATT CARLTON & THE WHEEL

Matterson (Matt) Carlton began his career as a potter at about age 12 in Benton, Arkansas. Benton, in the 1880s, was a small community boasting an unusually large number of potteries. Good local clays must have been abundant, as well as fuel to fire all the neighborhood kilns. It was there that Carlton received early instruction in the art of turning or throwing vessels by hand on the potter's wheel. It was something he put to good use during his long life, as he found work in the various local plants and later in Southern California.

In 1915, Matt Carlton, his wife, and six of their children relocated to Los Angeles. Matt found his first California employment at Pacific Clay Products, but was only there a short time before moving over to Bauer. It is not known if he started at Bauer as a turner or whether he worked into the position, but his special skills must have proved useful to Andy Bauer and his budding business. Probably other men preceded Carlton in the capacity of turner and eventually moved on, giving Carlton a shot at the job.

Around the time of Carlton's hiring, Bauer was either initiating or expanding artware production. Art pottery dominated the firm's display at the Panama-California International Exposition held in 1915–1916 in San Diego. There is a tangible difference in the award-winning matte green Rebekah vases of this early period and the ones most often associated with Carlton. Is it possible that his personal style evolved so much over the years that both versions can be attributed to him? This is an interesting question that may never be fully answered.

Other early artware pieces, like the California vase (the Rebekah without handles) and Venus vase, are also generally credited to Carlton, but may have been the creations of other turners who either preceded him or were his coworkers in the early years. It seems unlikely that the entire output of hand-thrown pottery from this period could be the result of one man's efforts. Just as

the Rebekah vase itself was not a form unique to Bauer (other early potteries produced similar vessels), any number of turners could have practiced their craft within the scope of what collectors recognize as the Bauer archetype.

Not much changed during the twenties with respect to Bauer's hand-thrown output, except glazes were often confined to the interiors of forms. Interior and exterior colors were limited to dark translucent shades of green, brown, and blue. The surviving cobalt blue wares are often quite appealing, but the thin murky tones of green and brown, in many cases, leave much to be desired. This is probably why the Bernheim brothers yearned for a reliable glaze chemist and found one late in the decade. When Victor Houser tested his lively colored glazes on examples of the stockpiled bisque, a whole new artware chapter for Bauer opened up.

It was after this breakthrough occurred that Matt Carlton seemed to burst forth as a creator of distinctive vessel forms. His Southern roots are still evident in the vases, bowls, and other utilitarian forms of the thirties, but his work often displayed a playful abandon, possibly the result of finding himself in a liberating climate for advancement. His signature twist-handled vases are a favorite among collectors. They were made in sizes ranging from under 6" to over 24" in height. His ability to throw forms of that stature was a feat in itself, but in addition, the preponderance of them would turn out to be majestic adornments suitable for any porch or patio.

The full-color spectrum that Houser perfected for the "ring" line was deployed on Carlton's myriad forms. Like "ring," they were produced exclusively at Bauer's original plant.

Occasionally Carlton would venture out, making public appearances to demonstrate his considerable prowess at the wheel. He even appeared briefly in the film version of *Lost Horizon.* Although his output of handmade pottery declined during the forties, he remained a productive Bauer worker until his retirement in 1946 at age 75.

It is amazing to me how Matt Carlton's reputation has grown since 1982, when his identity was first revealed in print. His pots now command huge sums of money, especially large, signature examples which are becoming scarce. Certain colors seldom show up on Carlton pieces. For instance, Houser's early "ring" burgundy and ivory are rarely observed and add value to any example.

A very unusual 9½" white handmade vase, attributed to Matt Carlton, $1,500.00+.

Variations of Matt Carlton's "signature" style vase. Left to right: 18½" in orange-red, $1,800.00+, 14¼" in delph blue (uncommon color), $2,500.00+, 12" in Chinese yellow, $1,200.00+.

An array of handmade Bauer artware from the wheel of Matt Carlton.

Top row: 10" carnation vase, jade green, $350.00; 12" Rebekah vase, Chinese yellow, $1,000.00+, 10¼" California vase, yellow, $500.00+.

Center: 6" x 8" striated fan vase, white (uncommon color), $500.00+; 6" ribbed fan vase, black, $500.00+; 4½" vase, green, $125.00; 5¼" ribbed vase in iron stand, orange-red, $325.00+; 5¾" carnation vase, green, $200.00.

Bottom: 9½" ribbed vase with folded & notched rim, green, $850.00+; 10" twist handled vase, green, $1,000.00+; 9½" twist handled vase, royal blue, $1,200.00+.

Matt Carlton's distinctive handmade artware.

Top row: 8" basket (uncommon shape), orange-red, $2,500.00+; 3¼" fan vase, delph blue (uncommon color), $300.00+; 9½" vase, orange-red, $650.00+; 10¼" lamp base (uncommon item), jade green, $900.00+.

Center row: 3" ruffled rim vase, Chinese yellow, $200.00; 3¾" ruffled rim vase, green, $200.00; 4" ruffled rim vase, not Bauer; 6" ribbed ruffled rim vase, green, $250.00; 6" ribbed vase, yellow, $400.00; 3¾" fan vase, orange-red, $200.00.

Bottom row: 8" carnation vase, yellow, $400.00; 9½" ribbed fan vase, royal blue, $650.00+; 7½" ribbed fan vase, yellow, $400.00; 9½" basket (uncommon shape), royal blue, $3,000.00+.

Matt Carlton oddities. Left to right: 12" smooth sided ruffled rim vase, Chinese yellow, $500.00+; 9½" fan-shaped vase with crimped sides, orange-red, $750.00+; 5½" fan-shaped flared bowl, jade green, $500.00+; 8¼" hybrid Rebekah twist handled vase, orange-red, $800.00+.

Matt Carlton items. Left to right: 2½" x 6" square bowl, orange-red, $150.00; 5½" smooth sided vase, jade green, $400.00; 6½" "upside down" California vase, $500.00+; 3½" x 7" ruffled rim bowl, jade green, $150.00.

Matt Carlton and family.

A pair of handmade twist handled ("hands on hips") vases by Carlton. Left: 16¼" in royal blue, $1,600.00+. Right: 15¾" in Chinese yellow, $1,400.00+.

Carlton artware. Left to right: 5¼" ribbed vase, royal blue, $450.00+; 2" matchholder, orange-red, $150.00; 4¾" ribbed vase, black, $750.00+; 3" Mexican ashtray, delph blue, $350.00+; 6" ribbed flared rim vase, jade green, $350.00.

Dennis Ashlock, photo

Two atypical Carlton creations. Left to right: 8¾" ribbed and pinched twist handled vase, jade green, $1,000.00+; 8½" ribbed flattened vase, jade green, $1,000.00+.

More handmade artware from Matt Carlton.

Top row: 7½" carnation jar, delph blue (uncommon color), $375.00+; 8" ribbed ruffled rim vase, delph blue, $400.00+; 2" x 3¾" candleholder, black, $300.00+; 3¾" vase, royal blue, $300.00+; 6" ribbed fan vase, black, $500.00+.

Bottom row: 12" ribbed ruffled rim vase, orange-red, $650.00+; 8" ribbed ruffled rim vase, black, $600.00+; 10" grooved fan vase with handles (rare shape), black, $1,500.00+.

MONTEREY TABLEWARE & PLANT TWO

The serious fire that struck the Bauer factory in the fall of 1935 cinched the deal. Watson E. Bockmon already had his sights set on the nearby bankrupt Batchelder-Wilson tile plant. He realized that the phenomenal success of the new "ring" line had opened up numerous possibilities for expansion of his business. Because the fire so disrupted the everyday operation of the old plant, the acquisition of a supplemental facility became a more pressing concern for him and others in management.

The purchase of the factory was a definite boon to the business. The plant, which added about 150,000 square feet under roof, was technically superior to the aging original Bauer structure. It contained a modern tunnel kiln, automatic dryers, and other equipment which easily facilitated development of additional new lines of dinnerware and artware. The first of the new wares produced was **Monterey.**

The basic **Monterey** tableware was designed by Louis Ipsen. Building upon the surprising success of his "ring" design, Ipsen fashioned this new line as a somewhat more stylish variation. Its pattern consisted of a series of subtly graduated rings separated in the center by a wide plain band. Plates and bowls had wide flattened rims; on plates the grooves were confined to this area, but on bowls they covered the entire flank. Victor Houser not only created new glazes for **Monterey** but also a sophisticated new clay body based on talc instead of the usual stoneware components. Houser's colors, which were more than a slight departure from his previous formulas, included Monterey blue, canary yellow, green, California

orange-red, turquoise blue, red-brown, burgundy, ivory, and white.

The #400 Monterey line made its debut in 1936 and instantly caught on with the buyers and public. Although not nearly as successful or enduring as the "ring" ware, it nevertheless found its niché and was produced until the early to mid-forties. Another Bauer designer, Ray Murray, contributed to the line shortly after his hiring in late 1937. He added the oblong trays and vegetable bowls, covered butter dish, gravy bowls, midget sugar & creamer with tray, cake plate, ashtray, low 6-cup teapot (with pistol-grip handle), console bowl (with detachable candleholders), and the refrigerator beverage dispenser. The hardest-to-find pieces include some of Murray's best: cake plate, console bowl, midget sugar & creamer set, refrigerator beverage dispenser, oblong relish plate, and ashtray.

Rare Monterey ashtray in Monterey blue, $200.00+.

*Monterey basics. Front to back: Cup, $25.00–35.00;
saucer, $8.00–12.00; 7½" salad plate, $15.00–22.50; 9"
dinner plate, $20.00–30.00; 10½" dinner plate, $40.00–
60.00. Not shown: 6" bread & butter, $10.00–15.00.*

Monterey oval items designed by Ray Murray.

*Foreground: 10" oval vegetable bowl, $65.00–95.00; 10" relish plate, $75.00–100.00.
Background, front to back: 10" oval platter, $45.00–65.00; 12" oval platter, $45.00–65.00; 17" oval
platter, $65.00–95.00.*

These Monterey footed fruit bowls are sometimes confused with "ring." Left to right: 9" fruit bowl, $100.00–150.00; 12" fruit bowl, $150.00–225.00.

Left to right: Monterey candleholder, $50.00–75.00; Monterey centerpiece with detachable candleholders, Monterey blue, difficult to find complete, $500.00+.

Bauer's Monterey ware.

Top row: Covered coffee server, $85.00–125.00; 6-cup teapot, old style, $100.00–150.00; 6-cup teapot, new style, $150.00–225.00.

Center row: Cake plate, pedestal base, $200.00–300.00; midget sugar, open, $20.00–30.00; midget creamer, $20.00–30.00; tray, $15.00–22.50; covered refrigerator beverage dispenser, $250.00–375.00.

Bottom row: 5" fruit bowl, $20.00–30.00; 6" fruit bowl, $20.00–30.00; 7" soup bowl, $40.00–60.00; 9" serving bowl, $65.00–95.00 (black, very rare, $300.00+); 11½" salad bowl, $85.00–125.00.

The Monterey midget creamer & sugar set is not easy to find complete with raffia-wrapped metal handle. Left to right: Sugar bowl, open, $20.00–30.00; tray, $20.00–30.00; metal handle, $50.00+; creamer, $20.00–30.00.

9" Monterey serving bowl in black glaze, very rare, $300.00+.

Jim Johnson loading ware into Plant Two's tunnel kiln, 1942.

More Monterey ware. Left to right: Large gravy boat, $60.00–90.00; small gravy/sauce boat, $60.00–90.00; tumbler, $15.00–22.50; shaker, $8.00–12.00; sugar bowl, $30.00–45.00; creamer, $15.00–22.50.

#200 HI-FIRE POTTERY: RING ADDITIONS & FRED JOHNSON VASES

Hi-Fire Pottery was a new line issued by the business in 1937 or 1938. It was produced at Plant Two on a semi-vitreous talc body developed by Victor Houser, hence the name **Hi-Fire.** While each of the lines produced at Bauer's Plant Two utilized the new clay body, this group of items implied the company's celebration of the fact. Actually the line was something of a catch-all that included various "ring" kitchen accessories along with a smattering of garden ware, related floral containers, and the hand-thrown vases of Fred Johnson.

Hi-Fire "ring" kitchenware included a nested set of mixing bowls (#12-36 with no inside rings), beating bowls (a carryover design from Plant One), custard cups (an alternate "ring" design originally produced at Plant One), pie plates with racks, beehive-shaped salt and peppers, ashtrays/nut cups with holders, and "ramekins." A "ramekin" is defined by *Webster's New World Dictionary* as: "(1) a food mixture; specifically one made of bread crumbs, cheese, and eggs, baked in individual baking dishes or (2) such a baking dish." Other "ring" ware in the **Hi-Fire** assortment: cylinder-shaped vases in 6", 8", and 10" sizes, jardinieres in 5", 6", and 7" sizes, and flower pots (with rolled rims) in 4", 5", 6", and 7" sizes.

Vases that were hand thrown on the wheel by Fred Johnson, and also by his son Jim, were the highlight of the line. Seven root designs with variations were produced. Profiles of most of the forms mimicked those which Fred had turned out while employed by Niloak Pottery in Benton, Arkansas, from 1904 (at age 12) to about 1934. Johnson had been instrumental in helping Niloak owner, Charles Hyten, perfect the recipe for the company's successful Mission (marbleized) pottery, although he never received credit for it. (Hyten patented the process without acknowledging Johnson.) This disappointment was a factor in predisposing his migration to California.

Another impetus was Matt Carlton's beseeching of Watson Bockmon to hire Johnson at Bauer. Carlton, who was Johnson's uncle, persuaded Bockmon to send Johnson a train ticket to Los Angeles.

After his arrival in Los Angeles in 1934, Fred was assigned to work alongside his uncle Matt at Plant One, throwing similar forms on the wheel at first. When Plant Two opened, he transferred there and subsequently created a group of handmade vessels that were very different from Carlton's. Jim Johnson's daughter, Brenda Johnson Escoto, related that her grandfather was a perfectionist: "Before this time, it had been the practice (at Bauer) not to glaze the bottoms of

Fred Johnson's hand-thrown 15" garden vase with handles in California orange-red, $1,500.00+.

most wares. Papa (Fred) insisted on all his work being done 'properly' and therefore, each piece made was as perfect as humanly possible. Dad (Jim), in his early years working with Papa, would carve 'buttons' from the bottoms [of the vases prior to glazing]."

This added step of indenting the bases on Fred (and Jim) Johnson's pots, has made identifying them much easier for collectors. It is not a difficult task, in most cases, to separate the Johnson line from that of Carlton, despite the fact that the output of both was unmarked. The two potters had very different styles and work ethics. Fred Johnson threw with great precision and refinement in a style more akin to the Orient than the tradition of his rural Southern roots.

The glazes found on Fred Johnson vases and rose bowls are those common to many other lines produced at Bauer's Plant Two. They include turquoise (the most common), green, light blue, dark (Monterey) blue, yellow, red-brown, white, black (rare), and orange-red. Orange-red glazed **Hi-Fire Pottery** was singled out in company catalogs as costing 50% more, which accounts for the shortage of Johnson wares in the color orange. I believe it is possible that Johnson vases may also turn up in the matte colors used on the concurrent **Cal-Art Pottery** line.

The balance of the Hi-Fire package consisted of cast floral containers. The most interesting of these were the flared-rimmed flower bowls with fluted sides that were made in at least three sizes. Also included in the line were dog and cat feeding bowls. The smaller cat bowl is especially difficult to find.

Fred Johnson

Dennis Ashlock, photo

Very hard-to-find 5" Hi-Fire cat feeder, turquoise, $1,000.00+.

Hi-Fire vases handmade by Fred and/or Jim Johnson.

Top row: 9" stock vase, olive green (probably by Jim Johnson), $100.00; 9½" vase, white, $165.00; 6" #214 vase, Monterey blue, $60.00; 9" #214 vase, green, $135.00.

Center: 7" #214 vase, green, $125.00; 4" rose bowl, Monterey blue, $55.00; 6" #214 vase, matte pink (unusual color), $65.00+; 6" rose bowl, white, $80.00.

Bottom: 7" #213 vase, turquoise, $85.00; 4½" vase, turquoise, $50.00; 7½" #214 vase, red-brown, $65.00; 7" #215 vase, turquoise, $85.00.

Hand-thrown Bauer artware by Fred and/or Jim Johnson.

Top row: 12½" stock vase, white, $200.00; 12½" stock vase, turquoise, $225.00; 14" stock vase, chartreuse (late period color), $250.00. Note: These three vases most likely are the work of Jim Johnson.

Center: 6" rose bowl, yellow, $50.00; 6" rose bowl, California orange-red, $65.00; 7" rose bowl, Monterey blue, $100.00; 5½" rose bowl, white, $45.00.

Bottom: 9" #213 vase, turquoise, $135.00; 9" #213 vase, red-brown, $125.00; 7" vase #213, black, $150.00+; 9" #214 vase, Monterey blue, $150.00.

Bauer's Hi-Fire Pottery.

Top row: 6" #211 deep flower bowl, turquoise, $45.00; 10" #211 deep bowl, Monterey blue, $85.00; 6" #209 low flower bowl, light blue (unusual color), $50.00; 8" #211 deep bowl, black, $100.00+.

Center row: 5" cast version #214 vase, marked "USA," California orange-red, $40.00; 1¼" x 4¼" handmade ashtray, Monterey blue, scarce item, $100.00+; 1" x 4" handmade ashtray, turquoise, scarce item, $100.00+; 3½" x 11" fluted flower bowl, marked "Bauer Los Angeles," white, scarce item, $200.00+.

Bottom row: 7" dog feeder, chartreuse (late period color), scarce item, $400.00+; 2" x 5½" bowl with center hole, marked "Bauer Los Angeles," white (unusual item, see right), $60.00+; 5" bulb bowl, red-brown, $35.00.

All three sizes of the very popular Hi-Fire "ring" cylinder vase. Left to right: 10″ size, white, $200.00; 8″ size, Monterey blue, $150.00; 6″ size, black, $200.00+.

Two Hi-Fire items that fit well with the regular "ring" line. Left to right: Pie plate, red-brown, $60.00; pie plate rack, $45.00; beater bowl, yellow, $60.00.

7" Hi-Fire #215 vase, black, $150.00+. Note: Black glazed Johnson vases are very scarce.

Two versions of the elegant Fred Johnson garden vase. Left to right: 22" vase with handles, turquoise, $1,000.00+; 18" vase without handles, $800.00+.

11½" Fred Johnson pitcher (ewer), red-brown, very unusual, $500.00+.

Rarely seen paper labels for Bauer Pottery. I have observed them only on Hi-Fire items.

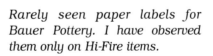

Left to right: 5" Hi-Fire slip-cast rose bowl, dark blue, $50.00; 5" #219 slip-cast vase, red-brown, $65.00.

CAL-ART POTTERY

Bauer's Plant Two was a beehive of activity in the late thirties. New lines were being developed and marketed in rapid succession. The arrival of Ray Murray in 1937 was a real boon to this burgeoning enterprise. Murray, who was 25 years old and a recent art graduate of the University of Oklahoma at Norman, had a brief stint (1935–1937) designing for Frankoma Pottery in his home state before moving to California. Hired by Jim Bockmon to make molds, his talent for modeling soon caught the attention of management, and he was promptly given free rein to design whatever he wished.

One of his initial projects was modeling an artware line called California Art Pottery, or simply **Cal-Art Pottery** when it was introduced in 1938.

All designs were slip-cast and encompassed vases, low flower-arranging bowls, jardinieres, flower pots, planters, candleholders, and Madonna figurines. Vases comprised the largest category — totaling at least 25 closely related designs. Many of the shapes displayed a modernist or Art Deco influence, but most were Murray's own spin on the traditional vessel form. His group of 5" "midget vases" was especially charming, though most were not marketing successes. These were supplemented by flower bowls, of which there were about 15 different shapes and sizes.

Additionally, three sizes of swan-shaped planters were produced, the largest being 13" in length, and two Madonna figurines, the taller measuring 10". The large statuesque Madonna was originally offered with an optional crescent-shaped light fixture, on which she stood. When lit, the light shined up onto her face. The metal fixture, which was painted white with a gold star in front, increased the price substantially, so only a few were ever made and sold.

Once again Victor Houser was called on to formulate new glazes. For the **Cal-Art** line he created six new matte colors: yellow, green, blue, white, dusty pink, and cream, in addition to turquoise blue and burgundy in regular gloss finish. As time went on, additional gloss-pastel colors found their way onto some of the more enduring items in the line. A few, like the swan planters and swirl pots, were produced well into the fifties, and can be found in the prevailing glaze colors of Bauer's final decade.

Ray Murray's departure in 1941 did not sound the death knell for **Cal-Art Pottery**. Modeler Tracy Irwin carried on the line, supplementing it to some extent. For instance, he added the larger scaled swirl pots and a sand jar in a similar scalloped design.

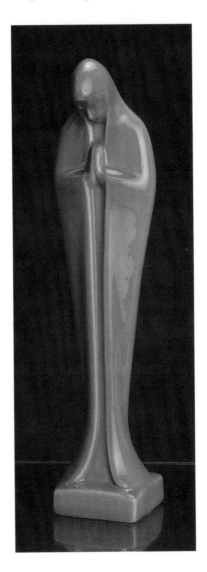

Certainly the most contentious numbers associated with the **Cal-Art** collection are the various small-scaled animal figurines. Only two of these are positively documented by virtue of their appearance in the widely circulated *Bauer 1941 California Pottery Catalog Reprint.* They are the Scottie dog and the hippo. Ray Murray vaguely recollected modeling the hippo. The Scottie was a precise reworking of an earlier die-cast model of unknown manufacture. This leaves in dispute a number of animal designs that have been found and attributed to Bauer. I am convinced that a few of these are the genuine article and have included them in a separate "Bauer Attributions" chapter. It is possible that Tracy Irwin was responsible for their creation. I believe that he modeled the set of three ducks that are the most commonly found of all the miniature animals. These ducks have turned up in many of the **Cal-Art** glazes and are occasionally found in other Bauer glazes like orange-red.

Dennis Ashlock, photo

Early 6½" wall pocket designed by Ray Murray in matte white, very rare, $400.00+.

Left to right: 10" Cal-Art vase, matte pink, $100.00; 9¾" square bowl, matte green, $45.00; 8" swirl bowl, matte green, $40.00.

Ray Murray's Cal-Art Pottery.

Left to right:
Top row: 9" vase, matte green, $80.00; 7" vase, matte cream, $85.00; 10" vase pitcher, matte yellow, $120.00.

Center row: 5" vase, matte white, $60.00; 4" midget vase, matte cream, $80.00; 4" "robot" midget vase, matte blue, $100.00; 5" vase, matte cream, $40.00; 4" midget vase, matte blue, $40.00.

Bottom row: 13" flower bowl, matte blue, $35.00; triple candlestick, matte white, $80.00; 3" x 9" swan, matte white, $85.00.

Cal-Art Pottery designed by Ray Murray.

Left to right:
Top row: 10" vase, matte green, $100.00; 8" Madonna, matte white, $200.00+; 10" Madonna, matte white, $250.00+; 6½" "horn of plenty" vase, matte blue, $45.00. Note: Madonna figures are scarce.

Bottom row: Low candlestick, matte white, scarce early item, $60.00+; double candlestick, matte white, $35.00; 2½" x 6" single oval candleholder, turquoise blue, $40.00; 10" oval flower bowl, matte blue, $45.00.

The Cal-Art swan clan designed by Ray Murray. Left to right: 3" x 9" medium swan, black (very rare color), $200.00+, other colors, $85.00; 2½" x 6" small swan (least common size), matte white, $100.00; 4" x 13" large swan, matte white, $150.00.

Bauer's California Art (Cal-Art) Pottery.

Left to right:
Top row: 8" vase, turquoise blue, $100.00; 6" "flat" vase, turquoise blue, $65.00; 7" vase, turquoise blue, $100.00.

Bottom row: 7" bud vase, matte blue, $75.00; 5" vase, matte blue, $35.00; 5½" x 7" vase pitcher, matte green, $65.00.

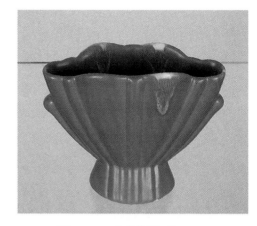

Cal-Art vases. Left to right: 4½" "flat" vase, matte blue, over-dripped, $50.00+; 7½" bud vase, burgundy (uncommon color), $85.00+; 7" bud vase, matte blue, $75.00.

Close-up of 4½" "flat" vase.

At left is an early 4" Cal-Art midget vase in seldom seen burgundy glaze, $100.00+. On the right is rare 6¾" "knot" bud vase in matte cream, $75.00. Note: Bud vase is similar to one originally produced at Frankoma by designer Ray Murray.

Cal-Art ware. Left to right: 7½" vase, matte white, $80.00; 8" vase, yellow (late period color), $75.00; 8" vase, matte white, $75.00.

Rare Cal-Art double cornucopia vase, matte blue, $200.00+.

Dennis Ashlock, photo

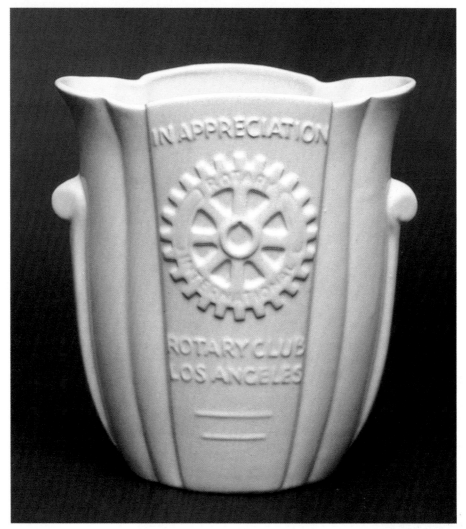

Dennis Ashlock, photo

A peculiar modification of an 8" Cal-Art vase #501, reading "In Appreciation/ Rotary Club Los Angeles" on front, matte white, $200.00+. Note: Bauer owners were Rotarians.

Dennis Ashlock, photo

Cal-Art miniature animals. Left to right: duck, orange-red (rare color), $100.00+; rare Scottie dog, matte white, $500.00+; rare hippo, matte cream (uncommon color), $400.00+. Note: Animals are usually found in matte white glaze.

The contentious three ducks in front of their wading pool.

Back: 10" flower bowl, pink inside/matte white outside (very unusual two-tone glaze is definitely Bauer-Los Angeles), $50.00+.

Front: 2¼" x 4¼" duck, matte green (uncommon color), $65.00+; 2½" x 3¼" duck (least common model), matte white, $50.00+; 4½" x 3" duck, orange-red (rare color), $100.00+. Note: Ducks are commonly found in matte white and are valued at $35.00–50.00.

BAUER POTTERY
LOS ANGELES

Marks typically found on Cal-Art ware.

LA LINDA TABLEWARE

La Linda tableware was another collaborative effort between seasoned veteran Louis Ipsen and the youthful Ray Murray. Like **Monterey,** this line was begun by Ipsen and enriched by Murray. The basic shapes were a throwback to Ipsen's original "plain" tableware with notable refinements.

The flatware that Ipsen modeled was not unlike his **Monterey** design — plates had wide flattened rims but there were no rings on them. Thus La Linda was another attempt at a smooth austere line from Bauer. Ipsen completed four plate sizes: 6" bread & butter, 7½" salad, 9" dinner, and 13" chop plate. The 9" serving bowl was nearly identical to the one included in his venerable "plain" line. Other La Linda bowls took their cue from this round rimless design: a 7" soup plate, a 6" cereal bowl, and a 5" fruit bowl were included. The remainder of Ipsen's contri-

bution to the line was an eight-ounce tumbler, a cup and saucer, a creamer and sugar, and salt and pepper shakers.

The new tableware was produced at Plant Two and introduced to the market in 1939 in four of the matte colors Houser had already created for Murray's **Cal-Art Pottery.** For some unknown reason its initial reception was luke-warm. Before leaving Bauer in 1941, Murray filled out the line as he had done earlier with **Monterey.** Added were 10" and 12" oval platters, 8" and 10" oval vegetable bowls, covered butter, gravy boat, and a remodeled creamer, covered sugar bowl, and shakers.

New glaze colors had to be formulated by Houser as a result of the wartime ban on various metals. In the process a new batch of lead-free gloss-pastel glazes were tested on the **La Linda** line. Houser did not think they were very good, since without tin, the standard opacifier, his new glazes tended to be thin. The public didn't seem to mind, however.

The glossy glazes transformed **La Linda** tableware into a bestseller for the company. The new colors included green, yellow, turquoise blue, pink, ivory, and brown. When Ray Murray created **Gloss Pastel Kitchenware,** some colors specific to this line were inadvertently (?) applied to **La Linda.** In the fifties, burgundy and gray replaced brown and ivory in the color selection.

The only **La Linda** piece that is truly difficult to find is the 8" soup plate. The rest of the line, especially in gloss finish, would be relatively easy to assemble into an attractive and useful dinner service.

La Linda basics. Note: Matte glazes at high end price scale.

Foreground: Cup, matte blue, $20.00; saucer, matte yellow, $8.00.

Background, front to back: 6" bread & butter plate, matte ivory, $8.00; 7½" salad plate, brown, $15.00; 9" dinner plate, green, $25.00.

At left is new style creamer designed by Ray Murray, pink, $15.00. At right is the old style creamer designed by Louis Ipsen, burgundy, $15.00. Note: Price difference reflects glaze preference only.

Bauer's La Linda dinnerware.

Top row: Tumbler, matte ivory, $20.00 (clip-on metal handle, $5.00); shaker, brown, $6.00; cup, yellow, $15.00; saucer, turquoise, $6.00; jumbo cup (scarce item), gray (late period color), $50.00+.

Center row: 6" cereal bowl, burgundy, $25.00; 5" fruit bowl, matte blue, $18.00; gravy boat, green, $25.00; gravy boat, matte pink, $35.00.

Bottom row: 12" oval platter, burgundy, $40.00; 10" oval platter, matte blue, $27.50; butter dish, matte pink, $75.00; 12" oval platter, matte yellow, $35.00; 10" oval platter, yellow, $25.00.

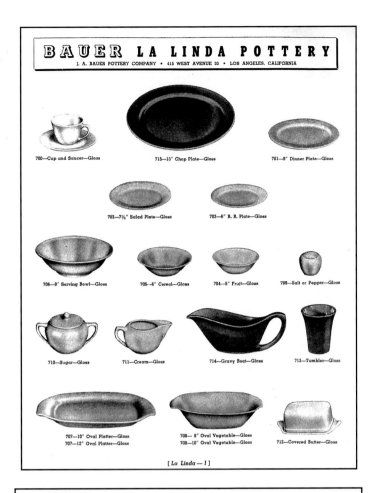

BAUER LA LINDA POTTERY
J. A. BAUER POTTERY COMPANY • 415 WEST AVENUE 33 • LOS ANGELES, CALIFORNIA

700—Cup and Saucer—Gloss

715—13" Chop Plate—Gloss

701—9" Dinner Plate—Gloss

702—7½" Salad Plate—Gloss

703—6" B. B. Plate—Gloss

706—9" Serving Bowl—Gloss

705—6" Cereal—Gloss

704—5" Fruit—Gloss

709—Salt or Pepper—Gloss

710—Sugar—Gloss

711—Cream—Gloss

714—Gravy Boat—Gloss

713—Tumbler—Gloss

707—10" Oval Platter—Gloss
707—12" Oval Platter—Gloss

708— 9" Oval Vegetable—Gloss
708—10" Oval Vegetable—Gloss

712—Covered Butter—Gloss

[La Linda — 1]

BAUER La Linda Tableware
2-FIRE GLAZED
PRICES IN EFFECT JUNE 16, 1941
This list supersedes all previous lists. Prices subject to change without notice.

GLOSS Colors: Green, Yellow, Turquoise Blue, Ivory, Pink and Brown.

BAUER
La Linda

JUNE 16,
1941

Stock No.				Retail Each	Wholesale Cost
700			Cup and Saucer	$ .50	$ .25
701	9	"	Dinner Plate	.50	.25
702	7½	"	Salad Plate	.32	.16
703	6	"	Bread and Butter Plate	.24	.12
704	5	"	Fruit Dish	.25	.12½
705	6	"	Soup or Cereal	.30	.15
706	9	"	Round Serving Bowl	.80	.40
707	10	"	Oval Platter	.80	.40
707	12	"	Oval Platter	1.00	.50
708	8	"	Oval Vegetable Dish	.80	.40
708	10	"	Oval Vegetable Dish	1.00	.50
709			Salt or Pepper	.35	.17½
710			Sugar	.50	.25
711			Creamer	.50	.25
710A			Sugar	.50	.25
711A			Creamer	.50	.25
712			Oblong Covered Butter	1.00	.50
713			8-oz. Tumbler	.30	.15
714			Gravy Boat	1.00	.50
715	13	"	Chop Plate	1.20	.60
717			6-Cup Tea Pot	1.20	.60
700			20-pc. Starter Sets	4.49	2.62

4 Cups, 4 Saucers, 4 9" Plates, 4 6" Plates, 4 5" Fruits.

The dealers buying above ware agree not to sell less than above retail prices.
No Allowance for Freight or Breakage.   Prices F.O.B. Factory
Packing charge varies approximately from 2 to 5% according to assortment packed.

J. A. BAUER POTTERY CO.
Bockmon's Hi Grade Stoneware, Flower Pots, Garden Pottery, Art Pottery
415-421 West Avenue 33 • Phones CApitol 4204-4205 • Los Angeles, California

Reproduced from Bauer's 1941 catalog.

RAY MURRAY'S GLOSS PASTEL KITCHENWARE

Gloss Pastel Kitchenware was the one line that Ray Murray could truly call his own. He created all the pieces in the line including a Bauer classic, the sleek and streamlined teapot known today as the "Aladdin."

Ray Murray

The **Gloss Pastel Kitchenware (GPK)** line was a fully coordinated ensemble of kitchen items designed to appeal to the modern home-maker. Unlike Louis Ipsen's use of compressed, regularly spaced ridges, Murray's concept embraced broader bands which subtly increased in width as they progressed upwards. The only smooth-sided pieces were the oblong, actually rectangular, bakers. In addition to teapots in 4- and 8-cup sizes, the line included a nested set of five mixing bowls, various sized pitchers, 1½-pint and 1½-quart casseroles with optional frames, cookie jar, batter bowl, beater bowl, custard cups, and ramekins with optional racks.

In Bauer's catalog, dated June 16, 1941, the **GPK** colors listed were green, yellow, light blue, dark blue, pink, and brown. Most items were available at that time in just four colors — green, yellow, pink, and brown. A good proportion of pieces were still in the general Bauer line when the company closed. Therefore, a variety of glaze possibilities exist for collectors. Very few speckled glazed examples have been observed, but many can be found in the solid gloss colors of the fifties — chartreuse, burgundy, gray, etc. Even black is a possible find, but be advised that a huge amount of bisque (unglazed) ware was left over when Bauer closed and some of it has been recently glazed black.

There are no items in the **GPK** line considered rare. The "Aladdin" teapots have become rather scarce these days due to their far-reaching popularity. The only other elusive articles would be the bakers.

Gloss Pastel Kitchenware cookie jar, yellow, $175.00.

Ray Murray's Gloss Pastel Kitchenware.

Left to right:
Top row: #12 mixing bowl, green, $50.00; #18 mixing bowl, brown, $45.00; #24 mixing bowl, light blue, $35.00; #30 mixing bowl, pink, $35.00.

Center row: 2-quart batter bowl, yellow, $65.00; 1-quart beater pitcher, pink, $40.00; 2-quart pitcher, yellow, $65.00.

Bottom row: 1-quart pitcher, ivory, $35.00; 1½-pint pitcher, pink, $25.00; #36 mixing bowl, yellow, $30.00; ramekin, dark blue, $10.00; custard cup, pink, $10.00.

Ray Murray's classic GPK teapot design, known to collectors as the "Aladdin." Left to right: 8-cup teapot, pink, $250.00+; 4-cup teapot, green, $150.00+.

GPK casseroles. Left to right: 1-quart size, olive green (late period), $45.00; 1½-quart size, light brown, $60.00; casserole frames, $20.00–25.00.

Luis Kopecky, proprietor of one of the many outdoor pottery outlets dotting California in the forties (this one located in Southgate), surrounded by an array of GPK items.

Gloss Pastel Kitchenware. Left to right: Ramekin, light blue, $10.00; custard cup, pink, $10.00; custard cup, dark brown (late period color), $10.00; custard cup, olive green (late period color), $8.00.

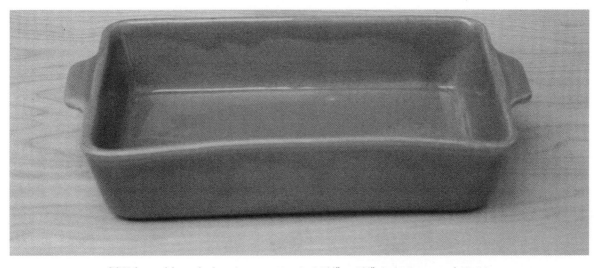

GPK low oblong baker (scarce item), 11½" x 6½", light brown, $45.00.

EL CHICO TABLEWARE: BAUER'S OWN RING LOOK-ALIKE

After its regional competitors got wind of the startling success of Bauer's "ring" ware, a rash of "ring" wannabes soon appeared. The competitive spirit was not surprising since most potteries in the thirties were suffering the ill effects of the recent stock market crash. Neighboring Pacific Clay Products was a prime challenger with its "Hostessware," followed by numerous others, some of which are featured in the "Bauer Look-Alikes" chapter.

Louis Ipsen joined in the mad rush to capitalize on the successfulness of **California Pottery** when his new tableware design called **El Chico** had its debut in 1939. It was a short set, which means it was a starter set comprised of basic place settings only. There was a 9" plate, a 7½" plate, a 6" plate, a cup and saucer, and a 5" fruit dish. That was all it amounted to. Conceivably, items from the regular line were to be used to supplement it. For instance, the #15 salt and pepper shakers go especially well with **El Chico**, as do any number of other objects in the extensive "ring" assortment.

Unfortunately, this rather nice line never got off the ground, as it appears to have been dropped from the company's production roster sometime prior to 1941. Even though it was an apparent refinement of the original, it was just too similar to the intensely popular "ring" pattern. Today, it poses a challenge to any collector who finds it appealing. Long ago I was able, with luck and perseverance, to complete a set in all the available colors: green, yellow, orange, dark blue, burgundy, and ivory — a feat I do not think I would attempt today.

The very elusive "ring" look-alike Bauer called El Chico.

Foreground: Cup, burgundy, $45.00+; Saucer, burgundy, $20.00+.

Background, front to back: 6" plate, orange, $20.00+; 8" plate, dark blue, $45.00+; 9" plate, ivory, $45.00+.

OIL JARS, SAND JARS & THE ELUSIVE BIRD BATH

Oil jars and sand jars are some of the largest and most prized items that Bauer manufactured. The oil jars especially seem to excite collectors, and the exotic and ancient lore surrounding them only adds to the excitement.

It would appear that oil jars were early additions to the general line, perhaps even precursors to the success of Bauer's **California Colored Pottery.** There were two dominant styles: the #100 jar, with its massive girth and prominent donut-shaped rim, and the #129 jar, which was more tapered and exhibited a somewhat flattened lip. Apparently, the #100 design came first and proved foremost in terms of sales appeal, considering the large number of surviving examples. The #129 jar is seen much less frequently today. This is rather remarkable since #129 stayed in the line for a much longer period. It was still listed in Bauer's Florist and Garden Pottery catalog as late as October 1, 1959.

The #100 oil jar was made in three standard sizes: 12", 16", and 22" heights. I have heard that a larger size may have been specially made for placement in movie theaters or similar locations. All sizes were jiggered in two sections and then pieced together with slip. The seam where the two sections were joined always remained visible and is a distinguishing mark. The colored glazes used at Plant One for "ring" dinnerware and kitchenware were utilized on the #100 jars, although some colors, like burgundy and ivory, are rarely seen. I do not know how the largest of these jars was dipped into Bauer's huge vats of glaze, but the process must have been a sight to behold.

The #129 oil jar came only in 20" and 24" sizes. They were made very much the same way as the #100 style and displayed similar seam lines. I believe the #129 oil jar was a Plant Two product because it turns up in the gloss colors that were used there exclusively. Because this design was still listed in the fifties, it also can be found in various speckled colors. Both the #100 and #129 jars are commonly found with no identifying marks on the bottom. It should be noted that Gladding McBean & Company of Lincoln, California, has issued a facsimile of Bauer's #100 oil jar. The 16" size jar was reproduced in the 1990s in numerous solid colored glazes and was listed as catalog item #1220.

Two handmade oil jars of the thirties. Left to right: 8" jar, jade green, $1,000.00+; 9¾" jar, Chinese yellow, $1,500.00+.

There is a third type of Bauer oil jar that was entirely handmade, not jiggered. I would say that these smaller scaled jars were the work of someone other than Matt Carlton or Fred Johnson, since very little resemblance exists between them and the work of Bauer's well-known wheel men. It does appear that they were produced at Plant One, though apparently not for long, as few have surfaced.

Sand jars make up another category of large scale ornamental pottery. Sand jars were used almost exclusively as receptacles for cigarette butts in the lobbies of hotels, theaters, and other public buildings. Many remain even today. They also make nice umbrella stands. Again, there were two designs. The straight-sided #122 sand jar was clearly the standard configuration, measuring 20" in height and 9" in diameter. As a rule, Bauer's sand jars were jiggered, but an entirely hand-formed example surfaces occasionally. The other style produced was the #124 swirl sand jar, a late addition to the line designed by Tracy Irwin. It measures 9" x 18" and may be found in both the solid and speckled colors of the fifties. However, it must be considered a rare find in any color.

Another rare find in any color would be the #126 bird bath. Measuring 22" in height with a 17" water tray, the elusive two-piece bird bath ranks as one of the hardest-to-find items in Bauer Pottery, if not the most difficult. It seems the extreme rarity is a result of two factors: limited sales and breakage. John Miali, a company salesman, recalled that the bird bath was always a hard sell for him because it was not an inexpensive article and tended to topple easily and break. Nevertheless, the #126 bird bath remained in the line for more than 20 years, so there must be some survivors.

Extremely rare 24" sand jar, #G101, pictured in Bauer's photographic catalog, circa 1929, could be ordered glazed blue, green, or yellow — Victor Houser's first three opaque colors.

Bauer's ubiquitous 20" sand jar, white, $400.00+.

Rare 22" hand-thrown stoneware sand jar, dark green, $800.00+.

Chris Witzke, photo

Bauer's majestic oil jars. Left to right: 24" #129 oil jar, jade green, $3,000.00+; 16" #100 oil jar, royal blue, $1,200.00+.

Bauer's stately ornamental oil jars in pre-World War II orange-red glaze. Left to right: 22" #100 jar, $2,000.00+; 12" #100 jar, $1,200.00+; 20" #129 jar, $1,500.00+.

One of the most elusive items pictured in Bauer's catalogs over the years is the 23½" x 18½" bird bath, shown here in speckled blue, $1,200.00+.

BAUER ATLANTA: The Wright Stuff

The Homer Laughlin China Company of Newell, West Virginia, sent a shock wave through the industry in 1936 when it introduced Fiesta, its answer to Bauer's **California Pottery.** Homer Laughlin was a very large company with a vast network of distribution throughout the country. Thus the success of Fiesta ware was immediate and widespread. Homer Laughlin's grip on the Eastern and Midwestern markets was especially strong, but Watson Bockmon believed these markets invited competition and hoped to somehow penetrate them. He had other motives too, so when the ideal (to him) situation presented itself in 1938, he purchased an abandoned winery in Atlanta, Georgia, with visions of widening his own ceramic empire.

A contingent of Los Angeles people was sent to Atlanta to help transform the place into a functioning pottery, which was no easy task, as the facility did not lend itself easily to the new purpose. Herb Brutsche, who eventually took over management, revealed that the two-story structure had no freight elevator. Consequently, ware that had been bisque fired in the ground floor kiln had to be hand carried upstairs before glaze firing. Eventually a makeshift hoist was constructed. This problem was only one of many that had to be solved.

Houser was sent to sample the local clays in hopes of finding one suitable for pottery manufacture, as well as to make certain his colored glazes would fit the new body. The initial plan was to get Bauer's popular "ring" ware into the major markets east of the Rocky Mountains.

In mid-1939, a few months after the official launching of his satellite plant, Watson Bockmon suffered a heart attack and died. Bernard Jackson, who had been supervising the modifications, returned to Los Angeles while Brutsche, considering it a challenge, took over as Atlanta general manager. Bob Manker then accepted the position of office manager. In addition to the hardships presented by the building itself, Brutsche had to contend with the outmoded equipment that thrift-minded Bockmon had insisted on installing.

It did not take long for Brutsche to realize that Bauer's "ring" line would never make serious inroads into the Eastern markets where Fiesta already dominated. The Homer Laughlin plant was an ultra-modern, fully automated facility capable of producing the same type of ware at a fraction of the cost. Therefore, his strategy was to focus all of the firm's energies in areas where it could be competitive: kitchenware, garden ware, and floral artware. Many of the same or slightly modified versions of kitchen items that had succeeded in the West were produced, such as mixing bowls, casseroles, cookie jars. Some of Ray Murray's **Cal-Art** pottery was attempted in Atlanta, with different glaze treatments. Some original designs were produced in an all-out effort to keep the business going.

As the United States involvement in World War II loomed ever closer, Brutsche began bidding on defense contracts. He was finally successful in the fall of 1941, and Bauer Atlanta got its first contract to produce simple china tumblers and cereal bowls for the military. Because so many of the minerals essential to successful production of colored glazes were declared off-limits during the war, the mainstay of the business became defense work. For the duration of the war, the Atlanta business contented itself with providing the Navy with humble, but essential, hotel-grade china utensils.

One of the two items made in Atlanta for the Navy during World War II was this sturdy china cereal bowl, $30.00. Not shown: similar 5½" tumbler, $35.00.

Brutsche's plant saw its most intense duty after the war as the company attempted a line of visionary **Russel Wright** artware. Brutsche was a big admirer of Wright's American Modern dinnerware, which had become the number one bestseller during the war years. A proposal was discussed with the designer that ultimately led to a manufacturing contract with Bauer Atlanta. Wright's own glaze chemist provided the unusual glaze formulas that were used on the 20 different cast models. The glazes were designed to run, but unfortunately they ran too much and serious setbacks, including damage to the kiln, occurred in the preparation of prototypes for the line's New York unveiling. Despite the difficulties, the **Russel Wright** artware was shown and the usual Wright buyers placed their orders. According to Brutsche, "After making the rounds of the gift shows, I think we wound up with 600 orders, but we only got one repeat order. I concluded that we were just about 10 years ahead of our time. The line looked good, but in most cases the stores didn't have the right furniture and furnishings to fit with the ware." The business lost thousands of dollars on the failed line and ended up liquidating a backlog of stock at give-away prices.

At the time the company was preparing to debut the artware of Russel Wright, his wife Mary proposed a tableware line of her own to Bauer Atlanta called **Country Gardens.** Prototypes were created based on her diagrams and color scheme, but fiscal disagreements over manufacturing vis-à-vis marketing resulted in the company not following through with production.

After the Wright debacle, Herb Brutsche strengthened his resolve to pursue an earlier plan of converting the Georgia business exclusively to sanitary ware production. Forming a partnership with Peerless Sanitary after its prosperous Indiana factory suffered a disastrous fire, Brutsche steered Bauer Atlanta in the direction of manufacturing toilets and lavatories under the tradename Georgia Sanitary Pottery in 1947. He continued to be an active shareholder in the business after his return to Los Angeles. Production of Georgia Sanitary finally ceased in the late seventies.

Bauer's loss with its **Russel Wright** artware has become a solid gain for those collectors lucky enough to find examples in the current marketplace. These items top the list of most coveted Bauer collectibles these days, due to their rarity,

Russel Wright's #3 corsage vase in an assortment of the glaze colors offered, $450.00+. Note: Certain rare glazes command much higher prices.

Adam Anik, photo

but mostly because the ware is appreciated now for the visionary achievement it was. The larger more exotic pieces are especially rare and command top dollar. Certain glazes and color combinations are similarly held in high esteem among aficionados. Mary Wright's **Country Gardens** is even more difficult to find than **El Chico.** Any example that turns up is truly a rare find! The balance of the Bauer Atlanta artware as well as its garden ware is relatively accessible, though not much is found on the West Coast. Unusual kitchen items, especially reworkings of familiar designs, are scarce and desirable additions to any Bauer collection.

Adam Anik, photo

Russel Wright Bauer. Clockwise from top: #14 tall candlestick, $600.00+; #4 jug vase, 9", $800.00+; #15 centerpiece with candleholders, $850.00+; #3 corsage vase, 5", $450.00+; #2 vase, 8½", $600.00+.

Adam Anik, photo

Bauer Atlanta's Russel Wright designed artware. Front to back: #8 ashtray, $400.00+; #19 bulb bowl, 8½", $750.00+; #1 pillow vase, $750.00+.

Russel Wright artware in Bauer's Atlanta brick glaze. Left to right: #13 round flower pot, 7", $500.00+; #12B square flower pot, 7½", $750.00+; #8 ashtray, $400.00+; #12A square flower pot, 4½", $350.00+. Note: #8 ashtray surfaces in slightly different forms.

Adam Anik, photo

Bizarre but beautiful Russel Wright designer items. Front to back: #8 ashtray, $400.00+; #11 "manta ray" centerpiece, 13", $1,500.00+; #9 mantelpiece bowl, 24", $850.00+.

Adam Anik, photo

Mary Wright's Country Gardens dinnerware was not officially produced, but samples occasionally turn up on the antiques market with high price tags attached. Clockwise from top: Large serving bowl, $200.00+; butter plateau, $250.00+; sugar bowl with spoon cover, $175.00+; 8" plate, $125.00+; cup and saucer, $125.00+; soup bowl, $125.00+; skillet server, $250.00+. Note: Certain rare glazes raise these prices considerably.

Adam Anik, photo

Adam Anik, photo

More Bauer Atlanta artware from designer Russel Wright. Front to back: #17 bowl, 11", $700.00+; #7 centerpiece, 17", $900.00+; #6 oval vase, 10½", $800.00+.

A sampling of Mary Wright's shelved Country Gardens line from Bauer Atlanta.

Top row: Open sugar bowl, spoon cover missing, $75.00+; open cruet, stopper missing, $75.00+; butter plateau, $250.00+.

Bottom row: Sugar bowl with spoon cover, $175.00+; creamer, $100.00+; cup and saucer, $125.00+; 6" plate, $75.00+.

Rare Country Gardens items designed by Mary Wright. Left to right: Sauce boat, deep, $200.00+; cruet with stopper, $175.00+; 8" plate, $125.00+; 6" plate, $75.00+; cup and saucer, $125.00+.

A selection of the general line of artware produced by Bauer Atlanta.

Top row: 14" lotus vase, $100.00; 11½" lotus vase, $65.00; 9½" lotus vase, $45.00; 8" lotus vase, $35.00.

Center row: 7" Cal-Art (mold) handled vase, $60.00; 7½" leaf formed ball vase, $80.00; 10" Cal-Art (mold) vase, $60.00.

Bottom row: 2" x 11½" Cal-Art (mold) low flower bowl, $20.00; 2" x 12½" Cal-Art (mold) low flower bowl, $25.00; 2¼" x 12½" Cal-Art (mold) low flower bowl, $25.00.

7½" fan-shaped vase by Bauer Atlanta, $80.00.

Two Bauer Atlanta pillow vases from Cal-Art molds. Left to right: 5½" vase, $40.00; 9" vase, $75.00.

Dennis Ashlock, photo

Non-Russel Wright Bauer Atlanta artware. Left to right: 7½" vase, $80.00; 10" vase, $85.00; 8" vase, $65.00; 6" x 11" double cornucopia vase, Cal-Art mold, $85.00.

A Bauer Atlanta modification, presumably by Ray Murray of his GPK "Aladdin" 8-cup teapot, rare, $250.00+.

Left to right: Bauer Atlanta ball jug, see mark on page 105, $200.00+; #18 mixing bowl, yellow, $60.00. Note: Bauer Atlanta "ring" mixing bowls have just two raised inside rings and are priced higher on the West Coast.

Bauer Atlanta translations of Los Angeles hits. Left to right: #12 GPK style mixing bowl, yellow-green, $45.00; 2-quart "ring" style pitcher, brown, $85.00. See marks on page 105. Note: Prices are higher on West Coast.

4" Bauer Atlanta flower pot, light blue, $20.00.

These Bauer Atlanta items appear to be modifications of the Monterey line. Left to right: Teapot, ivory, $150.00; butter dish, ivory, $100.00; tumbler, green, $25.00; tumbler, orange, $25.00; tumbler, ivory, $25.00; tumbler, dark blue, $35.00. Note: Prices are higher on West Coast.

BAUER *Pottery*
ATLANTA
U.S.A.

BAUER

ATLANTA U.S.A.

MARY WRIGHT

BAUER

Russel Wright

BAUER

MONTEREY MODERNE & RELATED KITCHENWARE

After Ray Murray's departure in 1941 and Louis Ipsen's death in 1946, Bauer was left with only one active designer-modeler, Tracy Irwin. Jim Johnson was an adroit modeler and mold maker, but his main aesthetic contribution to the business during its final decade was in glaze technology. Irwin already had helped model Herb Brutsche's **Al Fresco** dinnerware, so when Jim Bockmon gave his go ahead in 1948, he designed a similar line called **Monterey Moderne.**

Bauer's #800 **Monterey Moderne** dinnerware did not officially debut until 1949. It was a fully appointed line, when it was finally presented to the trade, having a variety of accessories to complement the basic service. The styling was modern — it was a coupe design with no rims to delimit generous portions or festive food presentation. The gloss colors were contemporary as well as complementary — yellow, green, brown, chartreuse, pink, burgundy, gray, and black.

In addition, a number of two-tone color combinations were marketed, consisting of a contrasting color topping or bordering monochrome glazed forms. Other unusual blended glazes were tested. Toward the end of the decade, a number of decal decorations were also offered. One consisted of a primitive barnyard scene and another one featured a more naturalistic epiphyllum spray. The extreme scarcity of these decal decorations suggests a very limited production.

A rundown of pieces in the line would include 9½" and 10½" dinner plates, 7½" salad plate, 6½" bread & butter plate, 4¼" fruit dish, 5¼" soup bowl, 8½", 10½", 13" serving bowls, 10" and 12" oval platters, 7" and 9" oval vegetable bowls, cup and saucer, salt and pepper, creamer, covered sugar bowl, covered butter dish, tumbler with optional clip-on handle, gravy bowl, chop plate, round and rectangular grill (divided) plates, two- and six-cup teapots, six-cup coffee pot, and 10-ounce mug. Sixteen-piece starter sets were also available. They wholesaled at $4.00 in 1958.

During the fifties, Irwin created an auxiliary kitchenware line that was produced in essentially the same color scheme as **Monterey Moderne.** A Bauer kitchenware catalog, dated January 2, 1956, pictured many of the pieces in this assortment. Available at the time were 1- and 2-quart batter bowls, one-pint pitcher, 1-, 2-, 2½-quart pitchers, 7", 8½", 10½", 13" low salad bowls, four-cup teapot, 4-, 5-, 6-piece mixing bowl sets, 10" pie plate with optional brass-finish frame, 14", 17", 19" Lazy Susan's, jumbo salt and pepper shakers, and 1-, 1½, 2-quart covered casseroles with numerous frame choices including a wicker basket. Some of the above listed items were available in speckled colors only.

Much of the **Monterey Moderne** dinnerware and companion kitchenware was still in production when the workers went on strike in 1961. A great deal of bisque (unglazed) ware was left over after the plant shut down, so be warned that recently glazed pieces, especially in black, are out there in the current marketplace.

Monterey Moderne basics.

Foreground: Cup, burgundy, $25.00; saucer, $10.00.

Background, front to back: 6½" bread & butter plate, olive green, $8.00; 7½" salad plate, gray, $12.00; 9½" dinner plate, burgundy, $25.00; 10½" dinner plate, pink, $30.00; chop plate, chartreuse, $50.00.

Bauer's Monterey Moderne dinnerware can easily be confused with Brusche Al Fresco.

Top: Mug without handle (Al Fresco 8-oz. tumbler), burgundy, $20.00; 10-oz. mug, black, $85.00+ (other colors, $30.00–35.00); mug without handle (Al Fresco 12-oz. tumbler), brown, $20.00; tumbler, gray, $20.00; metal handle, $5.00. Note: La Linda tumbler is same size and shape.

Center: Ramekin, $12.00; unusual cup without handle, pink, no price available; cup, burgundy, $25.00.

Bottom: 5¼" soup bowl, black, $50.00+ (other colors, $15.00–20.00); 7" serving bowl, chartreuse, $25.00.

Monterey Moderne salad/serving bowls. Front to back: 7" bowl, chartreuse, $25.00; 8½" bowl, olive green, $30.00; 10½" bowl, yellow, $35.00; 13" bowl, brown, $75.00.

Side view of salad/serving bowls.

Kitchenware made to complement the Monterey Moderne line.

Top row: 2½-quart pitcher, chartreuse, $85.00; 2-quart pitcher, burgundy, $85.00; 1-quart pitcher, brown, $50.00; 1-pint pitcher, chartreuse, $35.00.

Center row: 2-quart batter bowl, yellow, $50.00; 1-quart beater pitcher, burgundy, $50.00; 6-cup coffee pot pink, scarce item, $125.00+.

Bottom row: 6-cup teapot, yellow, $100.00; 2-cup teapot, black, $100.00+ (other colors $35.00–45.00); 5½" tall pitcher, brown, $35.00; 6½" tall pitcher, olive green, $45.00; 8½" tall pitcher, chartreuse, $75.00.

Do not confuse the Monterey Moderne 6-cup teapot, yellow, $100.00, with the very scarce original "plain" ware 6-cup teapot, orange-red, $300.00+. Note: This teapot design remained virtually unchanged throughout the history of the company.

Monterey Moderne round butter dish, pink, $65.00; salt or pepper, pink, $8.00 each; covered sugar bowl, chartreuse, $25.00; creamer, pink, $15.00. Note: La Linda round butter dish is same shape and size as Monterey Moderne.

12" Monterey Moderne platter, chartreuse, $35.00; 10" platter, brown, $25.00; 10¼" platter, likely Al Fresco, white (uncommon color), $30.00.

Bauer kitchenware of the fifties.

Top row: 8" canister / cookie jar, ceramic lid, chartreuse, $100.00; 6" canister, ceramic lid, olive green, $65.00; 7" canister, wood / metal lid (scarce item), olive green, $80.00+; individual casserole, chartreuse, $35.00; copper-plated metal frame, $20.00.

Bottom row: 1½-quart casserole, olive green, $40.00; brass finished metal frame, $15.00; 1-quart casserole, black, $80.00+ (other colors, $35.00); copper-plated metal / wood frame, $20.00.

Monterey Moderne and related kitchenware of the fifties.

Top row: #36 mixing bowl, burgundy, $50.00; #30 mixing bowl, gray, $35.00; #24 mixing bowl, yellow, $40.00; #18 mixing bowl, $50.00.

Center row: #9 mixing bowl, olive green, $75.00; #12 mixing bowl, chartreuse, $75.00; 9" oval vegetable bowl, chartreuse, $40.00; 7" oval vegetable bowl, olive green, $30.00.

Bottom row: 8½" divided vegetable bowl, brown, $45.00; three-tiered hors d' oeuvre tray, $75.00 (black 9½" plate adds to value); 8½" salad bowl, brown, $35.00.

The two decal designs attempted by Bauer in the late fifties. Left to right: "Epiphyllum Spray" on 10½" dinner plate, $30.00; "Barnyard Scene" on 4" x 4½" canister with wood/ metal lid, $35.00.

"Barnyard Scene" decal on Bauer kitchen items of the late fifties. Note: All items with "Barnyard" decals can be considered scarce.

Top row: Pillow vase (or canister without lid), $45.00; canister with wood/metal cover, $45.00.

Bottom row: Canister/cookie jar with wood/metal cover, $100.00; low salad bowl, $40.00; 7" canister with wood/metal cover, $85.00.

Cliff Coles, photo

Monterey Moderne and other lines were consolidated under the heading "Kitchenware" in speckled colors in the late fifties.

Top row: 2-quart batter bowl, pink, $45.00; 1-quart beater pitcher, blue, $35.00; 6-cup coffee pot, pink, $65.00; 1-quart pitcher, blue, $45.00. Note: 6-cup coffee pot came complete with brass finished candle warmer, $15.00.

Bottom row: Brusche 1-pint pitcher, yellow, $35.00; Brusche 2-quart pitcher, yellow, $50.00; 4-cup teapot, white, $50.00; 6-cup teapot, yellow, $60.00; 2-cup teapot, pink, $40.00.

MISSION MODERNE: A New Discovery

Bauer's **Mission Moderne** is an eleventh hour discovery! A dinnerware line closely related to **Monterey Moderne**, it bore stock number 400 (the old Monterey number) and was introduced sometime in the early fifties. Certainly the work of Tracy Irwin, it may have been created to capitalize on the success of **Monterey Moderne**, his prior dinnerware accomplishment.

As the accompanying sales brochure clearly illustrates, many of the same items were produced in **Monterey Moderne** and **Mission Moderne**, often with corresponding numbers. Differences between these two kindred dinnerware designs may be difficult to detect. One clue: **Monterey Moderne** and **Mission Moderne** coupe dinner plates are listed in corresponding brochures as 9½"/10½" and 10"/11" respectively. This size disparity can also be noted in the bread & butter plate and the fruit dish. An obvious design difference is observable in **Mission Moderne's** cups, sugar bowl, and creamer, which are more elevated and have distinctly pointed handles. These items, as well as others, were previously thought to be alternatives within the **Monterey Moderne** design. Not unlike **El Chico**, examples of **Mission Moderne** may go unrecognized or be confused with their counterparts in the current market.

Another differentiating feature of **Mission Moderne** is the divided vegetable bowl. Three sizes are listed: a 7" and 9" oval bowl and a 10" round bowl. The bowls tend to be deeper and the sides more angled, but a side-by-side comparison is needed to fully appreciate the acute subtlety.

Glazes might provide a means of separating the two lines. In February 1958, the **Monterey Moderne** colors were listed as green, yellow, chartreuse, pink, brown, gray, and black. The undated (but presumably same period) **Mission Moderne** brochure lists the colors available as dark green, chartreuse, burgundy, gray, yellow, and brown. Also listed are speckled colors of lime green, brown, yellow, turquoise, gray, and pink. It is evident that some solids were communal while others were not, at least in 1958. Since a certain amount of crossover occurred in glazing, by design or otherwise, a truly definitive accounting of Bauer lines can never be assumed, but this analysis, if categorical, does help in differentiating two very similar lines. Complicating the case is the existence of two-tone and blended colors, which can be found on examples of **Monterey Moderne** *and* **Mission Moderne**.

No. 400
Bauer Mission Moderne
J. A. BAUER POTTERY CO.

415 West Avenue 33

Los Angeles 31, California

COLORS: Dark Green, Chartreuse, Burgundy, Gray,
Yellow and Brown

SPECKLED COLORS: Lime Green, Brown, Yellow,
Turquoise, Gray and Pink

Monterey Moderne and Mission Moderne compared. Left to right: Monterey Moderne tumbler, black (uncommon color), $50.00+; 9½" dinner plate, pink, $15.00; 6½" bread & butter plate, gray, $8.00; Mission Moderne 6" bread & butter plate, chartreuse, $10.00; cup, blended dark green, $20.00; Monterey Moderne cup and saucer, black (uncommon color), $65.00+.

Two-tone colors were applied to both Monterey Moderne (and related Kitchenware) and Mission Moderne. Left to right: Tall kitchenware pitcher, turquoise/olive green, $65.00; Monterey Moderne cup, pumpkin/brown, $20.00; 9½" dinner plate, turquoise/olive green, $20.00; 7½" salad plate, turquoise/dark green, $15.00; 6" Mission Moderne bread & butter plate, chartreuse/brown, $12.50; Monterey Moderne creamer, pumpkin/brown, $15.00; Mission Moderne sugar bowl and cover, chartreuse/brown, $27.50.

Round and four-sided grill plates were listed in both Monterey Moderne and Mission Moderne sales brochures. Left to right: 10½" round style, $20.00–25.00; 8½" x 10½" four-sided style, $25.00–35.00, unusual matte white, $40.00+.

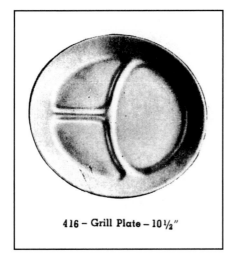

416 – Grill Plate – 10½"

416A – Square Buffet Plate

J. A. BAUER POTTERY CO.
415 West Avenue 33
Los Angeles 31, California

MISSION MODERNE PATTERN No. 400

**STOCK
No.   I T E M**

400	Cup & Saucer
400	Cup only
400	Saucer only
401	11" Dinner Plate
401	10" Dinner Plate
402	7½" Salad Plate
403	6" B. B. Plate
404	5" Fruit Dish
405	6" Cereal Dish
405	6½" Soup Bowl
406	7" Serving Bowl
406	8½" Serving Bowl
406	10" Salad Bowl
406	10" Round Divided Vegetable
407	10" Platter
407	12" Platter
408	7" Oval Vegetable
408	9" Oval Vegetable
409	Salt or Pepper
410	Sugar Bowl and Cover
411	Creamer
412	Covered Butter Dish
413	Tumbler
413	Handle
414	Gravy Boat on stand
415	13" Chop Plate
416	10½" Round Grill Plate
416A	Square Grill Plate
417	6-Cup Tea Pot
418	2-Cup Tea Pot
419	10-oz. Mug
428	7" Oval Divided Vegetable
428	9" Oval Divided Vegetable
400	16-Piece Starter Set

Carton Pack - 16-Piece Set

SOLID COLORS: Dark Green, Chartreuse, Burgundy,
Gray, Yellow and Brown

SPECKLED COLORS: Lime Green, Brown, Yellow,
Turquoise, Gray and Pink

BRUSCHE AL FRESCO & CONTEMPO

Al Fresco

Back home from wartime duty in Atlanta, but not the recipient of a hero's welcome when he returned to the parent factory in Los Angeles, Herb Brutsche soon realized that to produce a truly contemporary line of dinnerware in California he must rely on his own resources. Thus in 1948, after securing a small manufacturing facility in Whittier, he began an ill-fated production of **Al Fresco** ware as Brusche (the "t" was dropped) of California.

Brutsche, who was one of Russel Wright's many admirers, was eager to reap the rewards of his recent association with the master by consolidating some of Wright's design philosophy within his own project. He believed that Wright's engaging American Modern dinnerware had appealed to a different level of customer than the average Bauer buyer, and this was the constituency he targeted with his new **Al Fresco** ware.

Tracy Irwin was called upon to model the shapes from idea sketches provided by Brutsche. Victor Houser also moonlighted, providing the four glaze formulas that were used to debut the line — chartreuse, maroon, dark green, and gray. Brusche **Al Fresco** was introduced to the trade at the Fall Gift Show in Los Angeles in 1948. Help with pronouncing the abbreviated company name was furnished in handouts that advised, "Say Broo-shay." The number of wholesale orders was encouraging, and production proceeded fairly smoothly for about two years until Rose Hills Memorial Park, owners of the property where the pottery was sited, decided the plant was an eyesore and forced Brusche out.

The disruptive move to its new location in Glendale was something from which the business was unable to recover and eventually orders for the line had to be transferred over to Bauer. Meanwhile, **Al Fresco** got a big boost when it was featured in the Museum of Modern Art's Good Design exhibit at the Chicago Merchandise Mart in 1950.

A reproduced **Al Fresco** brochure pictures and lists most of the items in the line after it was merged with Bauer in 1950. The listed colors at the time were hemlock green, coffee brown, lime, olive green, misty gray, and dubonnet — fancy names for the same glazes Houser had created for **Monterey Moderne**. Collectors have tended to slight Brusche ware in the past, but this will change as other Bauer lines become more and more scarce. Already scarce in the **Al Fresco** assortment are the kitchen canisters — spice, grease, coffee, sugar, flour, and cookie jar.

In 1960, along with Herb Brutche's resurgence of influence in the Bauer organization, came a new lease on life for his **Al Fresco** line. It had become difficult for buyers to discern any differences between it and Irwin's **Monterey Moderne**, so a whole new roster of satin-finish glazes was provided by Jim Johnson and the line was re-christened **Contempo**. The latest color trends were taken into account for the selected scheme of indio brown, pumpkin, slate, spicy green, champagne white, and desert beige. Once again, the neutral colors — slate and champagne white — seem to be the most elusive today.

Al Fresco 2-quart ice-lip pitcher with unusual raffia-wrapped handle, dubonnet $150.00.

#142—17'' Lazy Susan—made from hard pressed wood with six ceramic inserts and one center casserole. Heat resistant and stain proof. Revolves smoothly on twenty-four steel ball bearings. Base in Maple finish. Inserts available in solid or contrasting colors— Price $15.00.

This three tier tid-bit set is the favorite of smart hostesses from coast to coast. The 5'' bowl on top was just made for salted nuts while the 8'' and 10'' plates on the lower tiers take care of hors d'oeuvres. Retailing in contrasting colors at $4.50.

#115 Gravy Boat—all colors.................................$3.00

#141—Colorful four piece Mixing Bowl set. These deep bowls are ideal for use with electric mixers. Sets in following size and color only $5.00.

9½'' Outside diameter – 5½'' Deep – Green
8'' Outside diameter – 5'' Deep – Lime
6¾'' Outside diameter – 4¼'' Deep – Grey
5½'' Outside diameter – 4'' Deep – Dubonnet

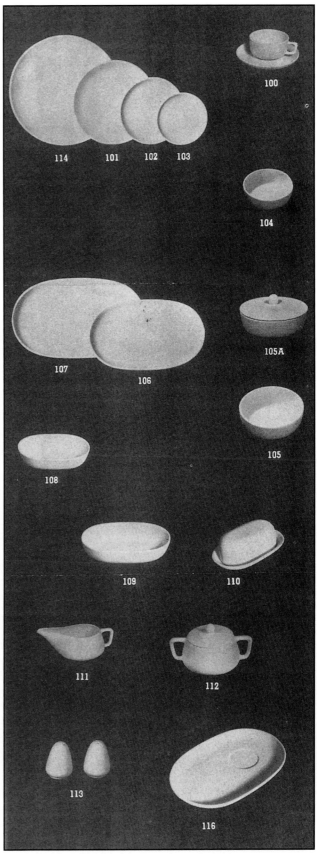

STOCK NO.	SIZE	DESCRIPTION	LIST PRICE
100		Cup and Saucer	1.00
100A		Cup Only	.60
100B		Saucer Only	.50
101	10"	Dinner Plate	1.00
101	11½"	Dinner Plate	1.50
102	8"	Luncheon or Salad Plate	.75
103	6"	Bread and Butter Plate	.50
104	5"	Fruit or Dessert	.40
105	5½"	Soup or Cereal	.60
105A	5½"	Covered Soup	1.00
106	10¼"	Platter	1.25
107	12"	Platter	1.75
108	7½"	Vegetable Bowl	1.20
109	9¼"	Vegetable Bowl	1.70
110		Covered Butter Dish	1.75
111		Creamer	1.00
112		Covered Sugar Bowl	1.10
112A		Cover Only	.30
113		Salt or Pepper	.50 ea
114	13"	Chop Plate	2.00
116	10¼"	Hostess Tray and Cup	1.75
117	6 Cup	Tea Pot	3.00
118	2 Qt.	Casserole	3.00
119	12 Oz.	Tumbler	.60
119	8 Oz.	Tumbler	.40
120	12 Oz.	Handled Mug	1.00
121	8 Oz.	Handled Mug	.60
122	2 Qt.	Ice Lip Pitcher	3.50
123	8 Cup	Coffee Server	3.00
124	13"	Salad Bowl	3.50
125	2 Qt.	French Type Casserole	4.00
126		Jumbo Size Creamer	2.00
127		Jumbo Size Covered Sugar	2.25
127A		Cover Only	.50
128	9¼"	Divided Vegetable Bowl	2.50
129		Individual French Casserole	1.50
130	4"	Coaster	.35
131	7½"	Round Vegetable or Serving Bowl	1.25
131	9½"	Round Vegetable or Serving Bowl	1.75
132	1 Pt.	Pitcher	1.25
132	½ Pt.	Pitcher	1.00
133		Jumbo Size Salt	1.25
134		Jumbo Size Pepper	1.25
		16 Piece Starter Set	8.00

THIS LIST EFFECTIVE
JANUARY 1st 1955

John Herbert Brutsche

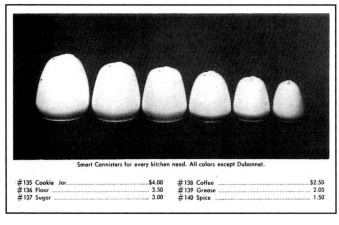

Smart Cannisters for every kitchen need. All colors except Dubonnet.

#135 Cookie Jar	$4.00	#138 Coffee	$2.50
#136 Flour	3.50	#139 Grease	2.00
#137 Sugar	3.00	#140 Spice	1.50

*Very rare canister set pictured in early Brusche brochure
dated November 20, 1950.*

Cliff Coles, photo

Brusché Al Fresco items.

Left to right:
Top row: 11½" dinner plate, 11½", lime, $12.00; jumbo salt & pepper, coffee brown, $15.00 each; 2-pint pitcher, misty gray, $40.00; 10¼" platter, lime, $20.00; jumbo creamer, dubonnet, $35.00; 2-qt. French casserole, dubonnet, $100.00.

Bottom row: Low cup & saucer, misty grey, $12.00; sugar bowl, hemlock green, $18.00; creamer, hemlock green, $15.00; 1-pt. pitcher, hemlock green, $35.00; 9¼" divided vegetable bowl, hemlock green, $30.00.

Brusché mark.

11¾" Brusché ashtray, high-style space age with 14-karat gold ball-shaped feet and cigarette rests, rare, $200.00+. Note: This item most likely not made at Bauer.

Contempo

Cliff Coles. photo

Brusche Al Fresco ware in speckled glaze colors.

Left to right:
Top row, background: 6" bread & butter plate, pink, $6.00; 8" lunch/salad plate, brown, $8.00; 10" dinner plate, gray, $10.00. Foreground: Sugar bowl, gray, $20.00; creamer, green, $15.00; 5" fruit/dessert bowl, yellow, $12.00; 5" fruit/dessert bowl, pink, $12.00; 5½" covered soup (cover not show), brown, $20.00; 5½" deep soup/cereal, pink, $15.00.

Bottom row: 7½" round vegetable bowl, yellow, $24.00; 9½" round vegetable bowl, yellow, $28.00; 9¼" oval vegetable bowl, brown, $26.00; 9¼" divided oval vegetable bowl, $30.00; 9½" round divided vegetable bowl, brown, $30.00.

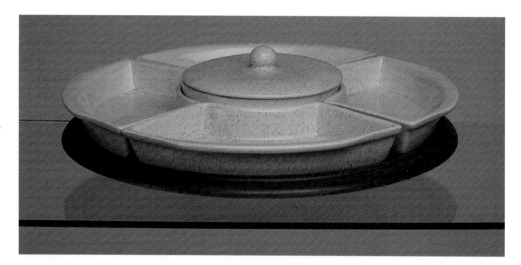

4" Lazy Susan, speckled yellow, 150.00 complete.

Cliff Coles, photo

Brusché dinnerware was also produced in speckled glazes and can be difficult to sort out from other speckled ware of the fifties. Note: Most of these individually named lines were consolidated into the general "Kitchenware" category by the late fifties.

Left to right:
Top row: Mission Moderne buffet plate, $20.00; Mission Moderne gravy bowl, $35.00; Cemar-Bauer square shakers, $20.00; Brusché jumbo shakers, $24.00.

Bottom row: Brusché 12-oz. handled mug $20.00; Brusché 8-oz. handled mug, $15.00; Kitchenware 8-oz. mug, $18.00; Brusché cup and saucer, $12.00; Monterey Moderne tumbler, $18.00; Brusché individual French casserole, $25.00.

Contempo 6-cup teapot, desert beige, $45.00.

Cliff Coles, photo

Left to right: Contempo 1-pint pitcher, Indio brown, $30.00; 8-oz. mug, pumpkin, $12.00; 6-oz. mug, was not part of the Contempo line, $10.00.

Cliff Coles, photo

Left to right: Brusche Contempo cup, spicy green, $12.00; 5¼" deep soup/cereal, pumpkin, $15.00; 6" bread & butter plate, $6.00; 10" dinner plate, $10.00.

TRACY IRWIN & THE FIFTIES

Bauer Pottery was beginning to slip in sales and standing as the fifties dawned. Tracy Irwin, who had started at Bauer in the early twenties, was the person most responsible at the time for modeling new ware or lines, and he made a significant contribution in keeping the business competitive, if not influential, during its final decade.

In addition to his **Monterey Moderne** tableware and assorted kitchenware, Irwin was very productive as an artware designer and modeler. The oft-cited *Florist and Garden Pottery* catalog of the late fifties – early sixties period pictured most of his designs. (See appendix.) Listed in order by stock number they included: #146 Indian bowl (two sizes), #504, 505, and 506 vases (eccentric shapes), #511 vase (two or three sizes), #513 pumpkin bowl (two sizes), #514 one-half pumpkin bowl, #515 bowl (similar pumpkin form fitted with brass-finish stand), #516 vase (three sizes), #517 bowl (similar angular form), #518 camellia bowl, #519 low bowl, #520 bowl (oblong, two sizes), #521 bowl (two sizes), #522 pedestal pot (and double pedestal pot), #521 and 522 combination pedestal and stand, #523 long bowl, #524 deep bowl, #525 fan vase, #526 bowl (pedestal base with matching candleholders), #528 long planter, #529 vase, #530 Grecian vase, #532 flower bowl (low, several sizes), #546 dome pot (several sizes with stands), and #1202 rectangular bowl.

These are the designs I feel most secure in crediting to Irwin. There presumably were others, but I will not attempt to single them out. A few of the above, like the Indian bowl, were adaptations. A sample was purchased and Irwin made a model or mold from it. In the case of the Indian bowl, someone brought in a true American Indian-made pot and suggested it as a nice addition to the line.

An interesting variety of glaze treatments was applied to the above listed items and others in the fifties. The most common of these glazes was the speckled glaze. This high-gloss glaze came in a wide variety of pastel colors — lime green, pink, turquoise blue, lemon yellow, gray, cocoa brown, and oyster white. Pink seems to be the most easily found, with lime green a close second. A second type of glaze that turns up on certain Irwin pieces is the satin-matte finish, featuring shades of green, beige, pink, turquoise, black, and white. Black once again is the most eagerly sought of the solids, while others, like turquoise, are much harder to find. Both types of glaze were furnished by Jim Johnson after he replaced Victor Houser in 1951. Bright gold was sprayed over the tops of some of these colors. The addition of 14-karat gold, which required a third firing at a lower temperature (until the gold fused with the glaze), must have been an afterthought, and not a particularly good one.

In 1960 or early 1961, prior to the Bauer walkout, an unnamed line (#300) of tableware and kitchenware was added to the Bauer inventory by Tracy Irwin. This truncated line echoed specific artware creations of the fifties, particularly his angular #516 vase. The ware was issued in a variety of glazes that included the Contempo palette and a new set of satin-matte speckled colors. Dinner plates resembled flower pot saucers, and in this respect Bauer tableware came full circle — Louis Ipsen's first design had also approximated them.

Cliff Coles, photo

Large 7" x 10" Indian bowl, matte black, fifties period, $200.00+.

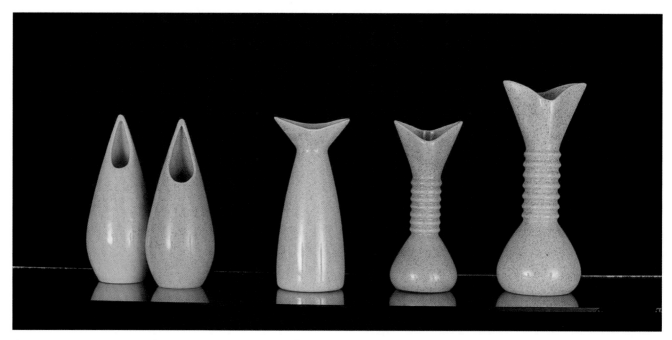

Irwin eccentrics in speckled colors. Left to right: 8" vase #505, green, $50.00; 8" vase #505, pink, $50.00; 8" vase #504, green, $50.00; 8" vase #506, pink, $50.00; 10" vase #506, white, $75.00.

Irwin designed artware at its best: 15" centerpiece bowl and matching candleholders in matte black $200.00+ set.

The popular Irwin pumpkin bowls. Left to right: 5" x 8" medium size, matte pink, $80.00; 4" x 6" small size, matte beige, $60.00; 7¾" half pumpkin bowl, matte green, $80.00.

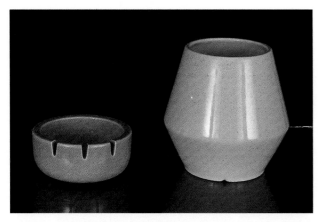

Ashtray, a copy of a popular Heath Ceramics design, speckled cocoa brown, $15.00; 6" vase, #516, speckled green, $35.00.

Large size pumpkin bowl, 6½" x 10", matte black, $150.00+.

Tracy Irwin designs.

Top row: 10" vase, #516, large size, matte turquoise, $85.00; 3½" x 6" bowl, matte yellow, $25.00; 8" pillow vase, matte white, $65.00.

Bottom row: #36 mixing bowl, desert beige, $20.00; custard cup, pumpkin, $10.00.

Dennis Ashlock, photos

I believe these three 10" vases are Tracy Irwin designs. Left to right: Vase, black, $150.00+; vase, matte black, $100.00+; fan vase, matte black, $150.00+.

This rarely seen 8½" x 14" pedestal bowl design by Tracy Irwin was listed in Bauer's late period price lists under the heading "Gardenware," matte yellow, $250.00+.

Cliff Coles, photo

Large size Indian bowl in speckled pink, $100.00.

Cliff Coles, photo

Indian bowls of the fifties with airbrushed 14-karat gold. Left to right: 6" x 7½" small size, matte beige, $80.00; 7" x 10" large size, matte white, $125.00; small, matte green, $80.00; small, matte beige, $80.00.

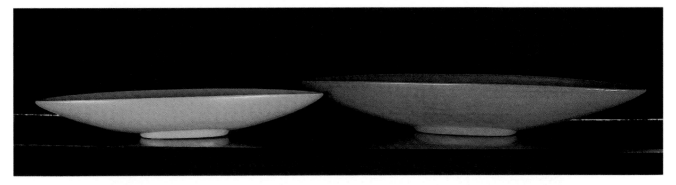

Tracy Irwin's 16" oblong flower bowl in matte pink, $40.00, and 20" oblong flower bowl in matte beige, $60.00.

Florist and garden pottery of the fifties in speckled glazes.

Top row: 20" oblong flower bowl, brown, $50.00; 16" oblong flower bowl, pink, $35.00. Bottom row: 8½" x 15" deep bowl, pink, $85.00; 12" stock vase, pink, $45.00.

This striking 16" Grecian vase, from the collection of John Herbert Brutsche, was introduced about the time the worker's strike ended most production, matte white with 14-karat gold outside, $500.00+.

Tracy Irwin's unnamed tableware line produced in the late fifties.

Irwin's unnamed kitchenware line items. Left to right: #18 mixing bowl, champagne white (gloss), $35.00; 4¾" diameter dish, yellow, $12.00; #12 mixing bowl, pumpkin (gloss), $45.00.

Cliff Coles, photo

Cliff Coles, photo

Artware of the fifties designed by Tracy Irwin.

Top row: 5" x 8" pumpkin bowl, medium size, matte black, $100.00+; 4" x 6" pumpkin bowl, small size, matte beige, $70.00; 10¼" half pumpkin bowl, matte black, $100.00+.

Bottom row: 6" x 16" rectangle bowl, matte white, $65.00; 18" long bowl, matte beige, $100.00.

APPENDIX:
ALL ABOUT PRICING

Most suggested prices appearing in this book are given in a spread, from low to high. A given price has its low end and its high end. If a price has a plus (+) after it then that price is the "bottom line" on a very rare or highly desirable item. With "ring," and certain other lines, the popularity of glaze colors determines the spread. Following this brief explanation of pricing you will find color spreads for the lines and types of ware in which color is a major determining factor in the price. If there is no spread for a given line, then the price would be the same for all colors.

It follows that the other factors influencing pricing are supply and demand and condition. The supply and demand situation is paramount! How abundant is the item in question? How much demand is there? These questions must be asked and answered if a reasonable evaluation is expected. Sometimes these factors are unknown, hence the suggested prices included in this book. But a keen awareness of the market in one's specific locale is very advantageous. Condition is the other major factor to consider. All prices given in this book are for items in mint or near mint condition only. Damage of any kind devalues an example, no matter how rare. How much devaluation depends on the type and extent of damage. A small chip is much less troublesome than a crack. Chips can be restored (or lived with) but a cracked piece has little usefulness and usually is not restorable. Crazing is a minor defect common to Bauer pottery. Uncrazed examples do command slightly higher prices, however.

There is also the grading factor to consider. Bauer ranked its ware either first or second grade. For some of its clients, only first grade merchandise was acceptable. The selling of discounted seconds was a specialty for others. Naturally most people prefer the best quality and condition available, but these days it is sometimes necessary to settle for less than the best owing to rarity. The grading question is only pertinent if the object in question is an obvious second, and devaluation is determined by the seriousness of the defect.

Grading Bauer's colors was one of the tasks I set before the seasoned dealers and collectors in my pricing survey. I got many different opinions but a definite trend did emerge and is reflected in the following color spreads. Color spreads are listed in ascending order of general collector preference.

CALIFORNIA POTTERY ("RING" & PLAIN WARE) Original pre-WWII colors: Light brown, Chinese yellow, orange-red, jade green (low), delph blue, ivory, dusty burgundy, cobalt blue (high), black (50% higher than high end), white (double high end)

CALIFORNIA POTTERY ("RING" & PLAIN WARE) Later post-WWII colors: Red-brown, olive green, light blue, turquoise, gray (low), chartreuse, "papaya," burgundy (high)

MATT CARLTON ARTWARE: Same as original **California Pottery** colors

MONTEREY: Red-brown, green, canary yellow, turquoise, ivory, California orange-red (low), Monterey blue, burgundy, white (high), black (double high end)

HIGH-FIRE and FRED JOHNSON ARTWARE: Same as MONTEREY colors

LA LINDA and GPK: Burgundy only high end color, but matte colors generally higher than gloss. Be cautious of black!

MONTEREY MODERNE and MISSION MODERNE: Only burgundy at high end, black double high end. Two-tone and blended colors at or near high end.

Color wheel consisting of original California Pottery colors. From top right: orange-red, jade green, delph blue, ivory, royal blue, dusty burgundy, white, Chinese yellow, and in center, black.

ADDITIONAL HANDMADE POTTERY

In addition to the work of Bauer's two "names," Matt Carlton and Fred Johnson, other handmade pottery materialized at the Los Angeles pottery. Positive identification of this other anonymous output is difficult even for the savvy collector. Reproduced in the following pages is an early photo album issued by Bauer, circa 1929, that reveals the unusual handiwork of someone only briefly associated with the business. Some forms are familiar, but many would not be readily recognized. Consequently bargains are possible if one is diligent.

Displayed in the first photo are the more familiar handmade articles, like the strawberry jar, with two sizes listed, 16" and 22". Also shown are oil jars and Rebekah vases. The oil jars came in two heights, 22" and 36", while the heights of the Rebekah vases are listed as 8", 10", 12", 14", 16", 18", 20", 22", and 24". It is likely that these items were hand thrown by Matt Carlton and possibly others employed at the time. They were available in "red" (unglazed red clay) or glazed blue, green, and yellow — Victor Houser's first three opaque colors.

The second photo represents three real oddities! Of these peculiar forms, only one or two examples of the Saxon vase have been observed. Houser remembers a (Mexican?) potter who was hired at about the same time he was, and that these could have been some of his pots. The Saxon vase came in 12", 14", 16", 18", and 20" sizes. The 18" goat vase and 13" water jug are most unusual and would be quite a find! All three samples pictured are listed as available only in red clay (unglazed bisque).

A third photo shows handmade flower pots. The Italian pot is familiar, as it later became a Bauer standard when it was adapted for jiggering. The other two designs are less familiar, although the Spanish pot did become a stock name. The sizes and colors available at the time are indicated under each pictured item. At the very bottom of a supplemental list of sizes and prices appear these portentous words: "Above are approximate sizes only."

Rare 12" Saxon vase, cobalt blue glaze inside, $1,000.00+.

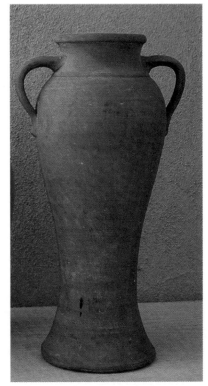

Rare 21" Rebekah vase, unglazed redware, $1,000.00+.

G 103
Strawberry Jar, Red
Also Glazed Blue, Green, Yellow
22" High
15 Cups

G 104
Oil Jar, Red
22" 36"
36" Red Only
22" Also Glazed Blue or Green

G 105
Rebekah Vase, Red
8"   14"   20"
10"   16"   22'
12"   18"   24"

G 106
Saxon Vase, Red
12"   18"
14"   20"
16"

G 107
Goat Vase, Red
18" High

G 108
Water Jug
13" High
Size 2

G 109
Glazed Flower Pot
Blue, Green, Yellow
3"   6"
4"   8"
   10"

G 110
Italian Pot, Red
8"   14"
10"   16"
12"   18"
   20"

G 111
Spanish Pot, Red
8"
10"
12"

FLORIST & GARDEN POTTERY

Left to right: 14" Italian pot, art pottery glaze #1 on red clay, $750.00+; 8" lion pot, orange-red, $300.00+.

Mark on bottom of Italian pot.

Left to right: 8" jardiniere with ruffled rim, made by Matt Carlton, black, $350.00+; 5" deco-style flower pot, rare early item, orange-red, $200.00+; 6" Indian bowl, black, $600.00+; 5" Italian pot, orange-red, $50.00.

Cliff Coles, photo

Three early and hard-to-find diamond-shaped stepped pots, $225.00+ each.

Left to right: Early 3¼" x 4¾" ring jardiniere, delph blue, $100.00+; standard 8" ring jardiniere, Chinese yellow, $275.00; 6" ring jardiniere, jade green, $250.00; 12" Biltmore jardiniere, delph blue, $250.00.

Left to right: 5" Hi-Fire ring-style jardiniere, yellow, $40.00; 5" pot saucer, jade green, $25.00; 6" Hi-Fire ruffle Italian pot, orange-red, $50.00; 8" pot saucer, black, $80.00+; 5" Hi-Fire step pot, yellow, $35.00; 10" pinnacle pot, olive green, $85.00.

Left to right: 8-cup cactus jar, handmade, 6" h x 12" d, green, $450.00+; 8" hanging basket, orange-red, $250.00.

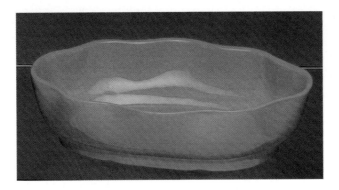

Oval bowl, 10½" long, Chinese yellow, $85.00.

Left to right: 9" 8-cup strawberry pot, burgundy, $200.00; 4" 8-cup strawberry pot, Chinese yellow, rare size, $150.00+; 9" 8-cup strawberry pot, white, $175.00; 4" 6-cup cactus jar handmade, jade green, $350.00+.

Hi-Fire Spanish pots.

Top row: 10" green, $100.00; 8" turquoise, $80.00; 7" dark blue, $80.00.

Bottom row: 6" black, $90.00+; 5" orange-red, low style, $45.00; 4" yellow and white, $25.00; 3" yellow and light blue, $15.00 each.

Left to right: 8" pinnacle pot, chartreuse, $75.00; Cal-Art jardiniere, 6" h x 8" d, matte white, $100.00; Cal-Art jardiniere, 8" h x 10" d, burgundy, $175.00.

Florist stock vases. Left to right: 18″ size, Chinese yellow, $450.00; 10″ size, jade green, $225.00; 6″ size, white, $150.00.

Cal-Art swirl pots.

Left to right: 7″ matte pink, $60.00; 6″ burgundy, $60.00; 5″ matte pink, $35.00; 4″ pink, $25.00; 3″ turquoise, $15.00.

In back: 5″ swirl jardiniere, green, $35.00.

Cliff Coles, photo

Florist and garden pots of the fifties in speckled glazes.

Top row: 7" square pot, pink, $40.00; 5"square pot, pink, $20.00; 5" rose bowl, green, $25.00; 3" Spanish pot, yellow, $12.00; 4" Spanish pot, white, $20.00.

Bottom row: 5½" low pot and saucer $30.00; 3¼" h x 6½" d make-up bowl, pink, $30.00; 6" pot/jardiniere, white, $30.00; 7" pot/jardiniere, green, $40.00; 4" pillow vase, green, $20.00.

Cliff Coles, photo

Bauer garden pottery in speckled glazes. Left to right: 20" sand jar, white, $250.00; 15" Biltmore jardiniere, brown, $200.00; 15" stock vase, green, $85.00; 16" oil jar, blue, $500.00+.

Cliff Coles, photo

More florist and garden pots in speckled glazes.

Top row: 7" pinnacle pot, green, $45.00; 5" pinnacle pot, pink, $30.00; 10" pinnacle vase, green, $75.00; 3¾" x 12" oblong pinnacle bowl, $40.00.

Bottom row: 4" x 24" oblong planter, green, $95.00; 5" swirl pot, green, $30.00; 5" swirl jardiniere, gray, $30.00.

Cliff Coles, photo

Fifties modern garden ware in speckled colors. Left to right: 9" pot/jardiniere, pink, $45.00, in brass finished stand, $35.00, $80.00 complete set; 5" dome pot, white, $30.00, in 5" brass finished three-prong stand, $30.00, $60.00 complete set; 11" dome pot, green, $80.00, in 10" brass finished ring stand, $50.00 (Note: This stand may not have been intended for this porticular pot); 12" swirl pot, blue, $100.00; 7" double pinnacle pot, green, $90.00.

Left to right: 7" Cal-Art swirl jardiniere, white, $60.00; 6" wide-banded Hi-Fire pot, white, $45.00.

Typical gardenware mark, usually combined with a size number.

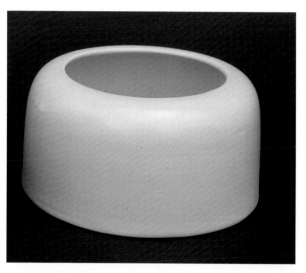

Florist make-up bowl in Brusche Contempo spicy green, $40.00.

Left to right: 15" bowl, speckled white, $200.00 (Not shown: brass finished stand, $75.00); 15" low bowl, green, $150.00.

Cliff Coles, photo

DECORATED BAUER: Gilding the Lily

Unlike most Southern California potteries, Bauer did not employ decorators to hand paint designs on its ware. Why then do collectors find so much hand-decorated Bauer pottery? The answer is simple: the ware, often seconds, was purchased from Bauer by artistic individuals and commercial studios, subsequently decorated, and frequently resold.

Examples from all periods of production have turned up with hand-painted scenes or other embellishments added over or under glaze, usually in oil paints. China painting was once a popular hobby, and Bauer dishes, although not true china (porcelain), have received a lion's share of decorative treatments over the years. I have chosen not to devote serious attention to this diversion since none of it originated at the Bauer factories. Because some examples were just too impressive to ignore, a few choice pieces are included here and elsewhere in the book.

The real focus of this section, however, is what seems to charm innumerable collectors and dealers, the white glazed kitchenware of the forties and fifties decorated with colorful fruit or stylized peasant figures. In the manner of the California Cleminsons, these objects bore homey hand-lettered phrases or descriptive monograms. Cookie jars and canister sets with wooden covers appear to be the most commonly found items. Investigation of this ware has yielded only sketchy information. I believe that the decorating was performed by Walter and Olga Klages at their studio located in Flintridge, California. Certainly a number of additional artists were involved in the work as the high volume would have been difficult for just two people to complete. It appears that some items produced were exclusives, as they were not part of the general Bauer line. No details regarding production dates or extent of distribution are presently known. All examples pictured here are from the collection of Joseph Smith and John Carlotti.

Cliff Coles, photo

Top row: Round butter dish, $125.00; tall shakers, $95.00 pair; small pitcher, $65.00.

Center row: Medium oval canister with wood cover, 6" x 6" x 4", $95.00; small oval canister with wood cover, 4" x 4" x 2¾", $65.00; medium oval canister with wood cover, 6" x 6" x 4", $95.00.

Bottom row: Large oval canister with wood cover, 8" x 8" x 6", $145.00; GPK pitcher, $85.00; GPK cookie jar, $300.00.

Cliff Coles, photo

Top row: Round butter dish, $125.00; GPK pitcher, $85.00; small canisters with wood covers, $65.00 each.

Center row: Large rectangular canisters without wood covers, $65.00 each.

Bottom row: Medium oval canister with wood cover, $95.00; large oval canister with wood cover, $145.00; medium oval canister with wood cover, $95.00.

Cliff Coles, photo

Top row: Small rectangular canister with wood cover, $65.00; large rectangular canister with wood cover, $85.00; small GPK pitcher, $85.00.

Center row: Small oval canisters with covers, $65.00 each; medium oval canisters with covers, $95.00 each.

Bottom row: Large oval canisters with covers, $145.00 each.

Cliff Coles, photo

Top row: Covered casserole/bean pot, $145.00; salt box with wood cover, $175.00.

Bottom row: Small round canisters with wood covers, $95.00 each.

Cliff Coles, photo

Cliff Coles, photo

Top row: Sugar bowl without lid, $40.00; 6-cup teapot, $245.00; underplate, $45.00; 2-cup teapot, $125.00.

Center row: GPK butter dish, $125.00; GPK beater bowl, $125.00; small flower pot, $40.00.

Bottom row: 8" plates, $95.00 each.

Top row: Round butter dish, $125.00; GPK pitcher, $85.00.

Center row: Medium oval canister with cover, $95.00; small oval canister with cover, $65.00; medium oval canister with cover, $95.00.

Bottom row: Large oval canister with cover, $145.00; GPK cookie jar, $300.00.

Cliff Coles, photo

Left to right: Ashtrays, $40.00 each; wall pockets, $85.00 each; Fisherman's Wharf souvenir ashtray, $60.00; ashtray, $40.00.

Low Dutch pitcher, handmade yellow ware with exceptional American Indian style decorations, signed "Kuykendall," $1,000.00+.

California Pottery line handled pickle dish, white with very fine floral decoration, $100.00+. Note: Undecorated white glaze, $200.00+ (other colors, $50.00–75.00).

Left to right: 6" yellow ware lamp base, handmade and hand decorated, signed "HNC," $500.00+; 16-oz. mug with polychrome Old Mexico decoration, $150.00+.

Individual bean pot, yellow ware with fine Art Deco-style polychrome decoration, $500.00+.

CEMAR TURNED BAUER

Left to right: 13" vase, speckled pink, $100.00; 5½" vase, speckled white, $40.00; 4" vase, speckled pink, $35.00; 9½" vase, speckled pink, $65.00.

Left to right: 5½" vase, speckled green, $40.00; 8¼" vase, speckled green, $50.00.

8½" Cemar-turned-Bauer vase, speck-led pink, $55.00.

2½" h x 8" d leaf bowl, Cemar-turned-Bauer, speckled white, $35.00.

A comparison of Cemar and Bauer versions of the same item. Left to right: Cemar original 5½" h x 12½" d leaf bowl, yellow, $40.00; Bauer interpretation, speckled pink, $60.00.

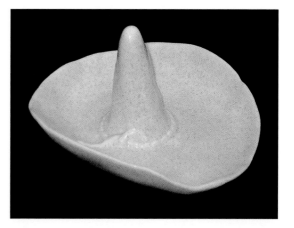

Scarce 6" Mexican hat ashtray, speckled green, $85.00+.

This cream pitcher, speckled yellow, $25.00, is closely related to the larger 20-oz. pelican pitcher (not shown), $45.00.

Bauer assigned multiple-uses for these bowls. Left to right: 12½" leaf bowl, speckled brown, $60.00; 13" heart bowl, speckled green, $55.00.

Cliff Coles, photo

Presently the most favored of the Cemar-turned-Bauer cookie jars is the fish shape, speckled blue, $150.00+.

Cliff Coles, photo

Cemar-turned-Bauer cookie jars.

Top row: Swirl shape, speckled pink, $85.00; jug shape, speckled brown, $85.00.

Bottom row: Churn shape, speckled green, $85.00; Candy jar shape, speckled pink, $85.00.

Listed here are items believed to have been made from the molds purchased from Cemar Potteries in the mid-fifties. The list probably is incomplete because catalogs did not specifically identify them. I am making my best reckoning based on years of observation and comparison of both Cemar and Bauer products. The items I believe Bauer put into production about 1955 are

#604	sugar bowl
#605	cream pitcher
#609	pelican pitcher
#644	leaf bowl, 9"
#645	leaf bowl, 11"
#646	leaf bowl, 12½"
#666	Western hat ashtray
#667	Mexican hat ashtray
#677	vase, 12½"
#678	vase, 10" and 13"
#679	vase, 6"
#680	vase, 4" and 7½"
#681	vase, 5½"
#682	vase, 9½"
#683	vase, 8½"
#684	vase, 8½"
#685	vase, 8¼"
#686	hors d'oeuvres
#687	flower bowl, 14"
#688	flower bowl, 14"
#689	flower bowl, 12"
#690	vase, 5½"
#814C	churn shape cookie jar
#815C	candy jar shape cookie jar
#816C	hexagon shape cookie jar
#821C	fish shape cookie jar
#823C	jug shape cookie jar
#823C	swirl shape cookie jar
#889	heart salad/fruit/flower bowl, 10" and 13"
#890	snack set (plate & mug)
#891	nut/candy basket

ACCESSORY METAL

Many items made by Bauer were provided with metal handles, racks, or frames. Some early handles were raffia wrapped while others were combined with wood. The earliest metal accessories were an integral part of many items in Bauer's popular **California Pottery** package. They were copper plated and often included wooden grips. Clip-on cup handles, sometimes referred to as "zarfs," were commonly used in the thirties and forties to complement the various lines of California pottery tableware. It is sometimes difficult to determine which were specifically made for Bauer.

Very little is known about the maker(s) of these early accessories, but they usually add usefulness and value to pieces when found. Some interesting metal parts are rarely seen and consequently highly prized. This category would include the "ring" salt and pepper holder, "ring" midget sugar and creamer holder, the holder for four ashtrays (square and round styles), the "ring" 10" and 12" chop plate handles (plain or raffia wrapped), the "ring" refrigerator jar frame, the "ring" ice bowl holder and tong set, and the fluffy beater for the "ring" beater bowl.

A newly uncovered brochure picturing ornamental iron stands and holders for flower pots, jardinieres, and other Bauer ware is reproduced here. The manufacturer of these items was Aztec Studios, and they were made for and apparently sold exclusively by the J. A. Bauer Pottery Company. No attempt will be made at this time to evaluate them individually, but all would qualify as valuable assets (and accents) to a Bauer collection.

In the fifties, Mirarmar of California manufactured decorative brass-plated casserole stands and warmers, coffee pot warmers, pie plate frames, ashtray stands, as well as frames and stands for planters and garden pots for Bauer. These also add completeness and value to

the appropriate ware when found. Of course, the value of these and the earlier copper-plated accessories would depend largely on their condition. The ravages of time and exposure to the elements can be hard on plated metal.

Chris Witzke, photo

Here is one of the most elusive of the "ring" line's metal accessories, the fluffy beater, which fits atop the beater bowl, $100.00+.

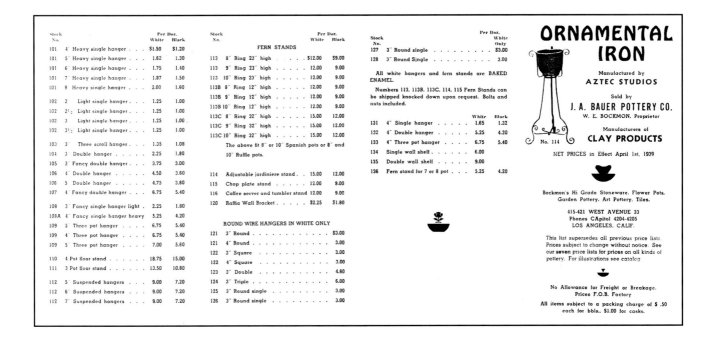

Stock No.		Per Doz. White	Black
101	4" Heavy single hanger . . .	$1.50	$1.20
101	5" Heavy single hanger . . .	1.62	1.30
101	6" Heavy single hanger . . .	1.75	1.40
101	7" Heavy single hanger . . .	1.87	1.50
101	8" Heavy single hanger . . .	2.00	1.60
102	2" Light single hanger . . .	1.25	1.00
102	2½" Light single hanger . . .	1.25	1.00
102	3" Light single hanger . . .	1.25	1.00
102	3½" Light single hanger . . .	1.25	1.00
103	3" Three scroll hanger . . .	1.35	1.08
104	3" Double hanger	2.25	1.80
105	3" Fancy double hanger . . .	3.75	3.00
106	4" Double hanger	4.50	3.60
106	5" Double hanger	4.75	3.80
107	4" Fancy double hanger . . .	6.75	5.40
108	3" Fancy single hanger light .	2.25	1.80
108A	4" Fancy single hanger heavy .	5.25	4.20
109	3" Three pot hanger	6.75	5.40
109	4" Three pot hanger	6.75	5.40
109	5" Three pot hanger	7.00	5.60
110	4 Pot floor stand	18.75	15.00
111	3 Pot floor stand	13.50	10.80
112	5" Suspended hangers . . .	9.00	7.20
112	6" Suspended hangers . . .	9.00	7.20
112	7" Suspended hangers . . .	9.00	7.20

FERN STANDS

Stock No.		Per Doz. White	Black
113	8" Ring 23" high	$12.00	$9.00
113	9" Ring 23" high	12.00	9.00
113	10" Ring 23" high	12.00	9.00
113B	8" Ring 12" high	12.00	9.00
113B	9" Ring 12" high	12.00	9.00
113B	10" Ring 12" high	12.00	9.00
113C	8" Ring 32" high	15.00	12.00
113C	9" Ring 32" high	15.00	12.00
113C	10" Ring 32" high	15.00	12.00

The above fit 8" or 10" Spanish pots or 8" and 10" Ruffle pots.

114	Adjustable jardiniere stand . .	15.00	12.00
115	Chop plate stand	12.00	9.00
116	Coffee server and tumbler stand	12.00	9.00
120	Raffia Wall Bracket	$2.25	$1.80

ROUND WIRE HANGERS IN WHITE ONLY

121	3" Round	$3.00
121	4" Round	3.00
122	3" Square	3.00
122	4" Square	3.00
123	3" Double	4.80
124	3" Triple	6.00
125	3" Round single	3.00
126	3" Round single	3.00

Stock No.		Per Doz. White Only
127	3" Round single	$3.00
128	3" Round Single	3.00

All white hangers and fern stands are BAKED ENAMEL.

Numbers 113, 113B, 113C, 114, 115 Fern Stands can be shipped knocked down upon request. Bolts and nuts included.

		White	Black
131	4" Single hanger	1.65	1.32
132	4" Double hanger	5.25	4.20
133	4" Three pot hanger	6.75	5.40
134	Single wall shelf	6.00	
135	Double wall shelf	9.00	
136	Fern stand for 7 or 8 pot . . .	5.25	4.20

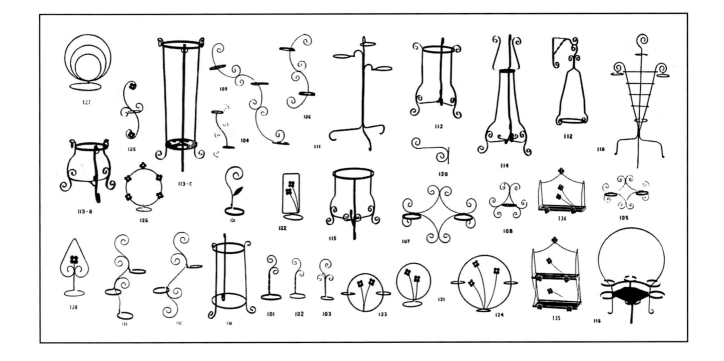

A practical iron holder for transporting a beverage set from kitchen to patio, $100.00+.

"Ring" items and their metal supporters. Left to right: Midget sugar and creamer holder, $50.00+. Copper finished and wood salt and pepper holder, $50.00+. Note: This caddy will hold any of the salt and pepper styles shown. Prices for shakers: El Chico style, $50.00 each; low "ring" style, $35.00 – 50.00 each (black, $60.00+); tall "ring" style, $35.00 – 50.00 each.

Non-plated wire rack for holding six custard cups, $30.00. Note: Prices for custard cups range from $25.00 – 35.00 (black, $75.00+).

The raffia-wrapped copper-plated chop plate handles came in two sizes, 10" and 12", $50.00+.

Cliff Coles, photo

Brass-finish (plated) frames and holders for fifties period kitchen items.

Top row: 1-quart (7½") casserole, speckled blue, $30.00, with frame add $15.00; 1½-quart casserole, speckled pink, $40.00, with frame add $20.00; 2-quart casserole, speckled pink, $50.00, with frame add $25.00.

Bottom row: 8" x 9½" buffet server, speckled yellow, $40.00, with buffet warmer add $25.00; coffee server with brass-finished holder, speckled green, $45.00; 1½-quart oval baker, speckled pink, $40.00, with frame add $20.00.

Left to right: 1½-quart casserole, speckled pink, $40.00, with frame add $20.00; 1½-quart oval baker, speckled yellow, $40.00, with frame add $20.00.

MISCELLANEOUS

Difficult-to-find Bauer Pottery post-World War II dealer sign, chartreuse, $1,000.00+.

This ashtray with raised Art Deco detailing and the inscription "Season's Greetings 1930/Bauer Pottery Co." was possibly a gift presented to valued customers, jade green, $500.00+.

Even more difficult to locate is this early pre-WWII Bauer Pottery dealer sign, green, $1,500.00+.

Sombrero ashtray, royal blue, $250.00.

These miniature pots ("school projects") were made by local school kids during tours of the pottery on weekends or after school, no price available.

Two Bauer vases that do not seem to fit within a specific line. Left to right: 5" h x 6½" d vase, jade green, $150.00; 4½" vase, turquoise, $200.00. Note: The turquoise vase is probably a product of Plant Two and seems related to the Monterey tableware line.

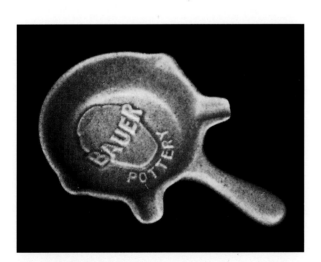

Bauer Pottery advertising ashtray of the fifties in satin matte speckle glaze, $500.00+.

This striking 7" x 7" vase bears a circular mark that suggests it was made in Atlanta, no price available.

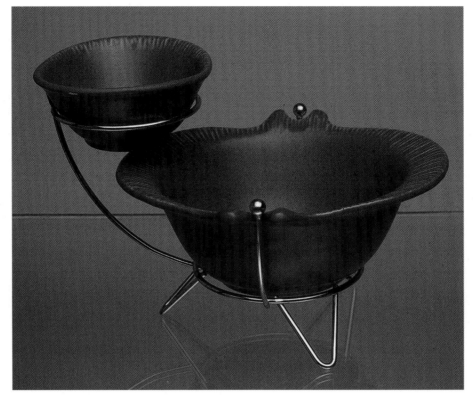

Cliff Coles, photo

From Bauer's stylish oven serveware line called Moonsong, late fifties to early sixties, comes this 7½" individual chip and dip set in Indio brown, $60.00 complete.

Cliff Coles, photo

Heath Ceramics look-alike ashtray from Bauer, pumpkin glaze, $25.00.

Cliff Coles, photo

This 3¾" advertising ashtray definitely was made in Atlanta after the plant's conversion to sanitary ware, $65.00+.

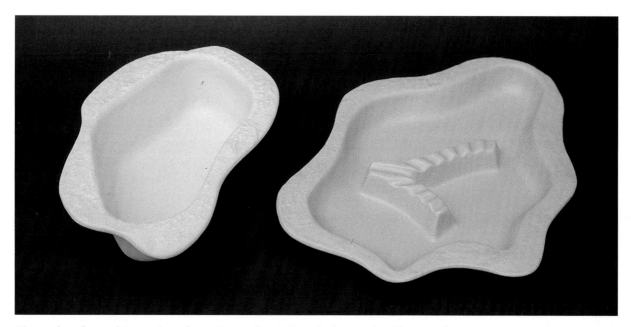

These free-form objects date from the early sixties. Left to right: Planter, champagne white (satin matte), $40.00; ashtray, Indio brown (satin matte), $40.00.

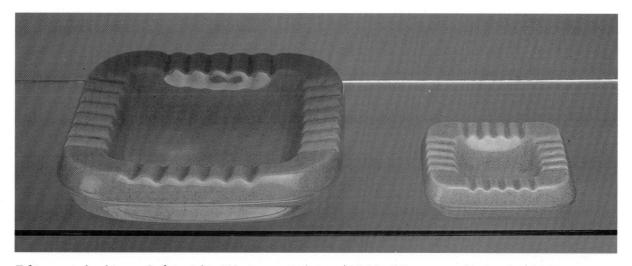

Fifties period ashtrays. Left to right: 11" size, matte beige, $45.00; 4½" size, speckled pink, $25.00. Note: 11" ashtray came complete with a brass finished stand with handle, $45.00.

This rare (medium rare?) open roasting dish measures 19" in length, speckled yellow, $100.00+.

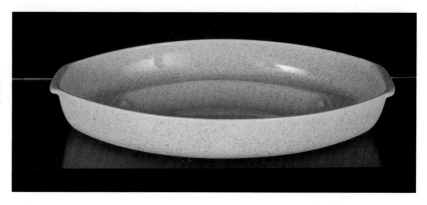

BAUER LOOK-ALIKES

The stunning success that Bauer achieved with its **California Colored Pottery** in the early thirties did not go unnoticed by the local ceramics trade. After the Wall Street collapse of 1929 and the ensuing economic upheaval, most pottery manufacturers in Southern California and elsewhere were hurting. Some had already or would soon experiment with colored pottery dishes and related articles as a means of surviving the Great Depression.

Not generally troublesome are the prominent companies that made comparable but distinctive lines and clearly marked them. What concerns the collector or dealer is the very similar but unmarked product of lesser-known potteries. Meyers Pottery, which was located in the industrial district of Los Angeles known as Vernon, produced an assortment of "ring" like dishes called California Rainbow. Anyone unfamiliar with this line could easily mistake it for Bauer ware. The similarities between Meyers and Bauer become apparent after studying the accompanying photos. Differences are more subtle but worth noting. California Rainbow items tend to be lighter in weight because its low fire clay was far less dense than Bauer's stoneware. Glaze discrepancies provide even greater clues for collectors as many of Meyers' glazes were semi-matte. But certain glazes, especially black, were a scrupulous duplication of Bauer's and could pose a problem for the unwary.

Another company that causes confusion, in California anyway, is Garden City Pottery of San Jose. The majority of this company's output of colored pottery was distributed locally so it mostly surfaces in the northern part of California. Since it could turn up anywhere, familiarity with it is important. The photos show Garden City items that bear a close resemblance to corresponding Bauer pieces. Because this company chose not to mark its extensive product line, any piece of dining or kitchen ware could cause confusion. Garden City also produced a great deal of garden pottery including oil jars. I always note numerous Garden City items mistakenly marked Bauer when I visit the antique malls of Northern California. Glaze differences again provide the best clue. The San Jose firm's colors are deeper and somewhat less opaque than Bauer's. Consequently, direct comparison of the two company's colors should lessen the risk factor.

Other misunderstandings surround Bauer's handmade pottery, especially the product of Matt Carlton. Although Carlton's ware was quite distinctive, the work of other potters is sometimes erroneously attributed to him. The Southern potteries, like Bybee and North State, cause the most confusion, considering Carlton's pottery heritage is rooted in the South. However, close comparison always renders notable differences. Panama Pottery of Sacramento is yet another company that produced hand-thrown art pottery which is sometimes credited to Bauer. This is my best advice: take the time to study and interpret distinguishing details of as much historical pottery as possible. Often it is just a case of one's awareness of how a company finished the base of its product. Is the base (bottom) glazed or not? Is it flat or indented? These small details often furnish significant information.

Thankfully, not many Bauer items were replicated in Japan. Shown is a "Made in Japan" sherbet dish, but the glaze is very thin and certainly a poor substitute for one of Houser's solid opaque colors.

California Rainbow

Garden City

Panama

Left to right: 14" vase, 10¼" vase, 10" vase.

At left is Matt Carlton's large handmade candleholder, 2½" x 7½", orange-red, $150.00+; on right is early handmade Brayton Laguna Pottery candleholder, 3" x 4".

At left is a 7" swirl pot made by Bauer's only real gardenware rival, U.S. Pottery of Paramount; on right is the genuine article. Note: The waves are wider and deeper on the Bauer pot.

Made in Japan model at left; Bauer on right.

I believe the 3¾" vase on the right to be a genuine Matt Carlton, but the 6" vase on the left is questionable since this item generally turns up in non-Bauer glaze colors. Perhaps it is a Pacific Clay product.

Garden City Pottery custard cup at left; Bauer on right.

BAUER ATTRIBUTIONS

A head positioned on the chopping block is always risky business, and I might be sticking my neck out somewhat in attributing certain items to the Bauer organization. I have proceeded anyway, knowing that a degree of risk is inherent in all endeavors.

Attribution is sometimes necessary because Bauer, like many a pottery manufacturer, failed to mark all of its product. The entirety of the company's handmade pottery was not identified by any form of base marking. Collector uncertainty can sometimes be resolved by simple comparison of an unmarked piece with a marked Bauer example. When this is not an option, the matter requires some detective work. Comparing glaze color and density, clay type, and other technical points in combination with aesthetics may yield an answer. Oftentimes, the clues do not add up to a definitive resolution. Barring the availability of paper evidence (company catalogs or other pictorials), designation of a questionable piece as genuine may be called for, but only as a last resort.

Attribution is not wish fulfillment! Declaring it does not necessarily make it true, even if one is considered an authority. Accordingly, I must submit that any number of attributions made here may be in error, even though I have taken care to examine and deliberate fully on each one.

Paper evidence is what is hoped for when controversy clouds attribution. Thanks to the diligent efforts of James Elliot and Patrick Barry of The Pottery Shop of Seattle, Washington, we now have some hard evidence to corroborate our crediting of the three miniature Cal-Art animals pictured in this section. Pictures would have been definitive, but the following text, excerpted from the December 1939 issue of *Ceramic Industry* (p. 31) is conclusive enough:

Bauer Adds New Ware

The J. A. Bauer Pottery Co., Los Angeles, Calif., has introduced a new starter set of dinnerware known as El Chico. This is made only in the four most popular vivid colors — orange, yellow, blue, and green... New figures added to the art pieces during the last few weeks, to be used largely for centerpieces for low flower bowls, include a hippopotamus, lion, horse, two different types of dogs, and a crane.

I strongly believe these three miniature animals belong with the other Cal-Art line animals. Left to right: 3½" x 5" lion, matte white, $500.00+; 4" x 4½" pony, matte white, $300.00+; 4" x 4½" collie dog, matte white, $500.00+.

This 3½" x 5¾" cowboy hat ashtray is widely accepted as made by Bauer, red-brown, $200.00.

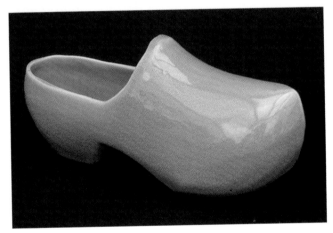

At left is an 11½" vase, matte white, attributed to Bauer, $85.00. Note: There also is a 9" size version of this vase. At right is a Tracy Irwin designed 4½" vase, matte black glaze, $50.00.

10½" Dutch shoe planter, green, $75.00.

REPRINTS OF CATALOGS & BROCHURES

Early Bauer

Pictured in the J. A. Bauer Pottery catalog reproduced here are most of the redwares and whitewares the company made in the twenties (and earlier). This was the heyday for the firm's white glazed jars and brown glazed jugs (pages 26–27), many of which were used by domestic brewers during the "dry" Prohibition years. Numerous kitchen items, such as bean pots (page 26), mixing bowls (pages 24–25), salt jars (page 23), milk crocks (page 29), and pitchers (page 29) are shown as well.

Stoneware products more likely to be found on the farm are pictured on page 30. A wide assortment of vases and jardinieres are presented on pages 7–11, while the many sizes of rose and carnation jars, which were used in abundance by local florists, are included on page 12. Other fancy designs in gardenware are pictured like the lion pot, royal pot, laurel wreath porch pot (page 14), the very popular Indian bowl, and hanging basket (page 15). These items were offered in a choice of dark green and dark blue glazes, which could be limited to the inside only.

Plain and fancy styles of redware flower pots are shown (pages 16–17), along with the more exotic Jap tubs and rustic stumps displayed on page 19. Redware ollas were used domestically to store and dispense drinking water (page 21). A fully outfitted Klean Kool Filter precedes page 7, the first page number recorded in these early Bauer catalogs (for good luck perhaps).

KLEAN KOOL FILTER

Combined Filter and Cooler.
Complete with Stand and Faucet.

HIGH QUALITY GLAZED POTTERY IN COLORS

10-inch   9-inch   8-inch

JARDINIERES

(See Cut below)

Made in sizes of 6 and 7 inches.

Green and Blue.

JARDINIERES (See Cut above)

Made in sizes of 8, 9 and 10 inches.

Green and Blue.

7-inch   6-inch

J. A. BAUER POTTERY COMPANY, Los Angeles, California   *Page Eight*

CALIFORNIA VASES

(See Cut below)

Made in sizes of 6, 8, 10, 12, 14, 16, 18 and 20 inches high.

Green, Blue, and natural colors.

VENUS VASES (See Cut above)

Made in sizes—
3x6 inches
4x8 inches
4x10 inches
5x12 inches
5x14 inches
6x16 inches

Green, Blue, and natural color.

Mission Vase   Bud Vase

MISSION VASES
   (See Cut above, at left)
   Made 9 inches high.
   In natural color only.

BUD VASES OR CANDLE-STICKS
   (See Cut above, at right)
   Made 8 inches high.
   In natural color only.

REBEKAH VASES (See Cut below)

Made in sizes of 8, 10, 12, 14, 16, 18, 20, 22 and 24 inches high.

Green, Blue, and natural color.

Los Angeles Vase   Steamship Vase   Peacock Vase   King Tut Vase
8 inch   6 inch   5 inch   4½ inch
Glazed inside only, outside colors optional.

HYACINTH JAR
CHINESE VASES

Octagonal or Round.
Glazed inside only, outside colors optional.

ROSE JARS (See Cut below)

Made in sizes—

2½x5 inches
3x6 inches
4x6 inches
4x8 inches
5x10 inches
5x8 inches
5x10 inches
5x12 inches
5x14 inches
6x8 inches
6x10 inches
6x12 inches
6x14 inches
6x16 inches
7x18 inches
8x20 inches
8x22 inches
9x24 inches

Green, Blue and
Natural Colors

CARNATION JARS (See Cut above)

Made in sizes—
4x6 inches
6x8 inches
6x10 inches
6x12 inches
6x14 inches
6x16 inches
7x18 inches
8x20 inches
8x22 inches
9x24 inches

Green, Blue and Natural Colors

MATCH AND
CIGAR
HOLDER
ASH TRAY

(See Cuts below)

Green and
Blue.

J. A. BAUER POTTERY COMPANY, Los Angeles, California   *Page Fourteen*

LION POT   **ROYAL POT**

Made in sizes 8, 10, 12,   Made in sizes 8, 10, 12,
14, 16, and 18 inches.   14, 16, and 18 inches.
Red, White, and Green.   Red, White, and Green.
Also Jardiniers Glazed   Also Jardiniers Glazed
Green and Blue.   Green and Blue.

**LAUREL WREATH PORCH
POTS** (See Cut at right)

Made in sizes 8, 10, 12 and
14 inches high; same
diameter.

Colors: Red and White.

Also made in Mat Green.
Glazed outside only).

Page Thirteen   HIGH QUALITY GLAZED WARE FOR DOMESTIC USES

FLOWER HOLDERS (See Cut below)

Made to match Flower Bowls, in 3 sizes.

In Green and Blue.   **DEEP FLOWER BOWLS** (See Cut above)
                                                Made in sizes of 5, 6 and 7 inches.

                                                LOW FLOWER BOWLS (See Cut below)

     Made in sizes of 5, 6, 8, 10 and 12 inches.
                                                Both styles in green and blue.

Page Fifteen   FINE GRADE NURSERY, PORCH AND GARDEN POTTERY

INDIAN BOWLS (See Cut below)

Made in sizes of 7, 8, 10, 12, 14, 16 and 18 inches.

(Also made in Green).

HANGING BASKETS (See Cut above)

Made in sizes of 7, 8, 9, 10, 12, and 14 inches.

Wire hangers extra.

J. A. BAUER POTTERY COMPANY, Los Angeles, California   *Page Sixteen*

HEAVY RIM FLOWER POTS

(See Cut below)

Made in sizes of 14 and 16 Fancy and Plain. 18 and 20 inches Plain Only.

FANCY RIM FLOWER POTS (See Cut above)

Made in sizes of 9, 10, 12, 14 and 16 inches.

FLOWER POT SAUCERS (See Cut below)

Made in sizes of 4, 5, 6, 7, 8, 9, 10, 12, 14, 16 and 18 inches.

(Also made in Green and White.)

Page Seventeen   FINE GRADE NURSERY, PORCH AND GARDEN POTTERY

FERN PANS (See Cut above)

Made in sizes of 5, 6, 7, 8, 9, 10 and 12 inches. 14 and 16 inch plain.

(Made also in Green.)

ENGLISH POTS

5x4½ inches
6x5½ inches
7x6 inches
8x7 inches

FLOWER POTS (See Cut below.)

Made in sizes of 1, 1½, 2, 2¼, 2½, 3, 3½, 4, 5, 5½, 6, 7 and 8 inches.

ROSE POTS

(See Cut above)

Made in sizes of 2½ and 2¾ inches.

J. A. BAUER POTTERY COMPANY, Los Angeles, California   *Page Eighteen*

VILLA VASES

(See Cut above)

Made in 14 inch diameter.

Colors: Red and White.

MONTECITO VASES

(See Cut above)

Made 14 and 16 inches in diameter.

Colors: Red and White.

Page Nineteen　　FINE GRADE NURSERY, PORCH AND GARDEN POTTERY

JAP TUBS

(See Cut below)

Made in sizes of 9 and 11 inches.

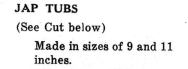

RUSTIC PANS

(See Cut above)

Made in 9x6 inches.

RUSTIC STUMPS

(See Cut above)

Made in sizes of 6x6½, 9x11 and 12x12 inches.

J. A. BAUER POTTERY COMPANY, Los Angeles, California　　*Page Twenty*

LOW SEED PANS

(See Cut below)

Made in sizes of 4, 5, 6, 7, 8, 9, 10 and 12 inches.

BED AND FOOT WARMER

Colors: White and Blue.

For use in sick room and hospital.

Page Twenty-one   FINE GRADE NURSERY, PORCH AND GARDEN POTTERY

OLLAS (See Cut above)
   With or without faucet holes.
   Made in sizes from 1 to 10 gallons.

  1 gal.—5½x10 inches
  2 " —7½x12 inches
  3 " —8x12¾ inches
  4 " —8¾x13 inches
  5 " —9¾x15½ inches
  6 " —9¾x16½ inches
  8 " —10¼x17
 10 " —11½x17¾ inches

FLUE THIMBLES

(See Cut below)

Made in all standard sizes.

J. A. BAUER POTTERY COMPANY, Los Angeles, California   *Page Twenty-two*

COMBINETTES—Complete
(See Cut below)
9¾x9 inches

CUSPIDORS

(See Cut above)

Made in 7 inch
Green and Blue,
glazed.

HOTEL CUSPIDOR

White, Green, Brown
a n d Blue. 7¼x4¼
inches.

CHAMBERS

9 inch, with or with-
out covers.
6 inch, without covers

HIGH QUALITY GLAZED POTTERY IN COLORS

SPICE JAR
Yellow and White glaze.
Made in 3 sizes—
No. 1—4½x3½
No. 2—6x4½
No. 3—6¾x5¾

SALT JAR
Plain
6x4 inches.

MARMALADE JAR
Yellow and White glaze.
Size 3x3¼ inches.

BEATING OR MAYONNAISE JAR
Size 5¼x4¾ inches.

CUSTARDS
Made in two sizes.
3½x2½ inches
4x2¾ inches.
Yellow and Brown.

RAMEKINS
Made in individual size only.
Yellow and Brown.
3½x1¾ inches.

J. A. BAUER POTTERY COMPANY, Los Angeles, California

STANDARD YELLOW MIXING BOWLS
(See Cut above)
Made in Nos. 36s, 30s, 24s, 18s, 12s, 9s, 6s, 4s, 3s, 2s, and 1s.

Outside Measurement
Across Top
No. 1—16 inches
No. 2—15 inches
No. 3—13¾ inches
No. 4—12½ inches
No. 6—11½ inches
No. 9—10¼ inches
No. 12—9¼ inches
No. 18—8 inches
No. 24—6¾ inches
No. 30—5¾ inches
No. 36—5¼ inches

ICE WATER COOLERS
Made with separate ice container.
Faucet extra. 4, 5 and 6 gal.

FINE YELLOW WARE FOR DOMESTIC USES

No. 6—11½ inches
No. 9—10½ inches
No. 12—9¼ inches
No. 18—8¼ inches
No. 24—7 inches

YELLOW MIXING BOWLS, RIM DESIGN (See Cuts above)
Made in sizes of 6s, 9s, 12, 18s, 24s.

YELLOW PUDDING DISH
(See Cut below)
Made in 6 sizes—
No. 1—5¼ inches
No. 2—6¼ inches
No. 3—7½ inches
No. 4—8¼ inches
No. 5—9¼ inches
No. 6—10¼ inches

16-oz. Mug   Approx. 12-oz. Mug—Hand Made

STRAIGHT SIDE NAPPIES (See Cut below)
Made in sizes 5, 6, 7 and 8 inches.

J. A. BAUER POTTERY COMPANY, Los Angeles, California   *Page Twenty-six*

BEAN POTS

(See Cut at right)

Individual 2¼x3 inches
1 pt.—3½x3½ inches
1 qt—5x3¾ inches
2 qts.—5x4½ inches
3 qts.—5x5⅜ inches
4 qts.—5x6¼ inches
8 qts.—5x10½ inches

JUGS, BROWN GLAZED
(See Cut at right)

Height—
1 pt.—5 inches
1 qt.—6½ inches
½ gal.—9 inches
1 gal.—10½ inches
2 gal.—12½ inches
3 gal.—15 inches
5 gal.—17 inches

HIGH QUALITY GLAZED POTTERY IN COLORS

1 lb.—3¼x4¾ inches, open only
3 lb.—5x5 inches, open only
5 lb.—5¾x5½ inches, open only
½ gal.6x6½ inches
1 gal.—7¾x7¾ inches
2 gal.—9x9¾ inches
3 gal.—10¼x10¾ inches
4 gal.—11¼x12½ inches
5 gal—12¾x13 inches
6 gal.—12¾x14½ inches
8 gal.—14¾x15 inches
10 gal.—14¾x17 inches
12 gal.—17x17¼ inches
15 gal.—17¼x20½ inches
20 gal.—19¼x20½ inches

WHITE GLAZED JARS AND COVERS

Also same sizes drilled for faucet.

(See Cuts above and on page 29)

Made in sizes of ½, 1, 2, 3, 4, 5, 6, 8, 10, 12, 15, and 20 gallons.

J. A. BAUER POTTERY COMPANY, Los Angeles, California

MILK CROCKS, WHITE GLAZED

See Cut at right)
Made in sizes of ¼, ½,
1, 1½ and 2 gallons.
¼ gal.—7x3¼ inches
½ gal.—8½x4 inches
1 gal.—10½x4½ inches
1½ gal.—12x5½ inches
2 gal.—12¾x6 inches

CHURNS, WHITE GLAZED (See Cuts below
Made in sizes of 1, 2, 3, 4, 5 and 6 gallons.

CHURNS

1 gal.—6x10 inches
2 gal.—7x12¾ inches
3 gal.—7¾x13¾ inches
4 gal.—9¾x14½ inches
5 gal.—9¾x17 inches
6 gal.—9¾x18 inches

PRESERVE OR PICKLE JARS WITH COVERS

(See Cut below)

½ gal.—5x7 inches
1 gal.—5x9 inches
2 gal.—5x10½ inches
3 gal.—5x12½ inches

Page Twenty-nine   HIGH QUALITY WHITE GLAZED WARE

1 lb.—4¾x2¾ inches
2 lb.—5½x3 inches
3 lb.—6x3¾ inches
4 lb.—6¾x4 inches
5 lb.—7¾x4½ inches
1 gal.—9x5¼ inches
2 gal.—11¾x6¾ inches

PITCHERS (See Cut below)

Sizes 30s and 12s. Approximately 1 and 2 quarts. White, Yellow and Blue mottled.
No. 30—4¼x5¼ inches
No. 12—5x7¼ inches

LOW BUTTER JARS, WHITE GLAZED

(See Cut above)

Made in sizes of 1, 2, 3, 4 and 5 pounds, also 1 and 2 gallons. Covers extra.

FUMIGATORS

(See Cut above)

Made in 1, 1½, 2, and 3 gallons. Brown glazed.

J. A. BAUER POTTERY COMPANY, Los Angeles, California   *Page Thirty*

RABBITT FEEDERS (See Cut above)

Made in Nos. 1, 2, 3 and 4 or 5, 6, 7 and 8 inches.

CHICKEN FEEDERS (See Cut below)

Made in sizes of ½ 1 and 2 gallon

CHICK FOUNTS
1 qt.—6½ inches high, 5¼ inch diameter
½ gal.—7½ inches high, 6 inch diameter
1 gal.—9¼ inches high, 7¼ inch diameter
2 gal.—12 inches high, 9 inch diameter

SAUCERS
1 qt.—7½ inches   1 gal.—10 inches
½ gal.—8½ inches   2 gal.—13 inches

½ gal.—9x3½ inches
1 gal.—13½x3½ inches
2 gal.—15x4¾ inches

SANITARY CHICK AND PIGEON FOUNTS (See Cuts above)
Chick Fount, made in ¼, ½, 1 and 2 gallons.
Pigeon Fount, made in ½ and 1 gallon.

Florist and Garden Pottery

By

J. A. BAUER POTTERY CO.

ORIGINATORS AND MANUFACTURERS OF
CALIFORNIA COLORED POTTERY

415-421 West Avenue 33 · Los Angeles 31 · California
Telephone: CApitol 5-4204

New York Showroom · **261 Fifth Ave.** · **New York 16, New York**

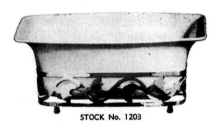

STOCK No. 1203
OBLONG PLANTER

SIZE	EACH
11" x 6"	$1.35
BRASS FINISH HOLDER	.85

STOCK No. 1204
SQUARE POT

SIZE	EACH
7" x 7"	$1.35
BRASS FINISH HOLDER	.85

STOCK No. 1205
OVAL BOWL

SIZE	EACH
10" x 5"	$1.10
BRASS FINISH HOLDER	.85

STOCK No. 1206
OVAL BOWL

SIZE	EACH
9" x 3½"	$ .95
BRASS FINISH HOLDER	.85

STOCK NO. 1207
OVAL BOWL

SIZE	EACH
13" x 5"	$1.35
BRASS FINISH HOLDER	.95

STOCK
No. 546
DOME POT

5"	$ .65
6"	.80
9"	2.20
11"	3.30
14"	4.90

STANDS

5"	$ .30
6"	.30
9"	1.55
11"	1.65
14"	2.20

SPECKLED COLORS
Lime green, Brown, Turquoise,
Oyster White, Pink

Page 1

Prices Net F.O.B. Factory, Los Angeles, Calif. and Subject to Change Without Notice

PLANTERS, BOWLS and VASES

STOCK No. 504
VASE

SIZE		EACH
8"	High	$ .65
10"	High	1.00

STOCK No. 505
VASE

SIZE		EACH
8"	High	$ .65
10"	High	$1.00

STOCK No. 506
VASE

SIZE		EACH
8"	High	$ .65
10"	High	$1.00

STOCK No. 677
VASE

SIZE		EACH
12½"		$2.00

STOCK No. 683
VASE

SIZE	EACH
8½" High	$ .85

STOCK No. 684
VASE

SIZE	EACH
8½" High	$ .85

STOCK No. 685
VASE

SIZE	EACH
8¼" High	$ .85

STOCK No. 687
FLOWER BOWL

SIZE	EACH
14"	$2.00

STOCK No. 148
BOWL

15" Wide, 7½" High..................$3.85
Brass Finish Stand............................ 1.75

STOCK No. 212
ASH TRAY & STAND

11" Wide, Complete....................$3.50

STOCK No. 507
OBLONG BOWL

12" Long, 3¾" High $1.50

Page 2

J. A. BAUER POTTERY CO.   415-421 W. Ave. 33

Items on Pages 1, 2 and 3 are made in the following
SPECKLED COLORS ONLY: LIME GREEN, PINK, OYSTER WHITE.

UNLESS OTHERWISE SPECIFIED.

STOCK No. 678	STOCK No. 679	STOCK No. 680	STOCK No. 681	STOCK No. 682
VASE	**VASE**	**VASE**	**VASE**	**VASE**

SIZE EACH
10" High....$1.00
13" High....1.25

SIZE EACH
6" High.....$ .40

SIZE EACH
4" High .....$ .25
7½" High..... .45

SIZE EACH
5½" High....$ .35

SIZE EACH
9½" High....$ .75

STOCK No. 688
FLOWER BOWL

SIZE EACH
14" $2.00

STOCK No. 689
FLOWER BOWL

SIZE EACH
12" $1.50

STOCK No. 690
VASE

SIZE EACH
5½" High..................$ .60

  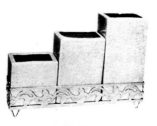

STOCK No. 508
ROUND BOWL

7" Wide, 3½" High..............................$ .70
8½" Wide, 3½" High.............................. .85
10" Wide, 3½" High.............................. 1.00

7" Brass Finish Frame ....$ .55
8½" Brass Finish Frame .... .60
10" Brass Finish Frame .... .70

STOCK No. 510
OBLONG PLANTER

18" Long, 4" High.....................$3.85
24" Long, 4" High..................... 5.50

18" Brass Finish Frames.....................$1.65
24" Brass Finish Frames..................... 2.20

STOCK No. 542
PILLOW VASE FRAME
ONLY

For 3 No. 542 Vases...........................$1.35
For 4 No. 542 Vases........................... 1.65
542—4 Vase................................... .45
542—6 Vase................................... .65
542—8 Vase................................... .85

Page 3

Los Angeles 31, Calif. · **CApitol 5-4204**

Items on Pages 4, 5, and 6 are made in the following SPECKLED COLORS ONLY unless otherwise specified: LIME GREEN, PINK, OYSTER WHITE.

*No. 103 is made in SOLID COLORS ONLY: Chartreuse, Olive Green, Yellow, White.

**No. 122 SAND JAR is made in SOLID COLORS: Chartreuse, Olive Green, Yellow, Grey, Black. SPECKLED COLORS: Lime Green, Yellow, Pink, Blue, Oyster White.

All Pots, Bowls and Vases, previously made and not shown in this folder, have been discontinued.

STOCK No. 980
THREE PRONG STAND

SIZE	Baked on Super Black Finish EACH	Brass Finish EACH
6"	$1.10	$1.30
7"	1.20	1.35
8"	1.30	1.55
9"	1.45	1.65
10"	1.55	1.75

The above are made to fit our Stock No. 1240 Pots.

STOCK No. 540
SWIRL POTS

SIZE	EACH
3" Swirl Pots	$ .20
4" Swirl Pots	.35
5" Swirl Pots	.50
6" Swirl Pots	.65
7" Swirl Pots	.90
8" Swirl Pots	1.10
10" Swirl Pots	1.65
12" Swirl Pots	2.50

SOLID COLORS: Olive Green, Yellow, White, Chartreuse, Black

SPECKLED COLORS: Lime Green, Grey, Pink, Oyster White Turquoise, Yellow.

STOCK No. 1240
NEW POT OR JARDINIERE

SIZE	EACH
6"	$ .65
7"	.90
8"	1.10
9"	1.35
10"	1.65

SPECKLED COLORS ONLY: Lime Green, Grey, Pink, Blue, Oyster White Yellow, Brown

STOCK No. 880
LOW RING STAND

SIZE	Baked on Super Black Finish EACH	Brass Finish EACH
6" Opening	$1.10	$1.10
7" "	1.10	1.35
8" "	1.10	1.45
10" "	1.20	1.55
12" "	1.40	1.65
15" "	1.55	1.75

The above will hold our Stock No. 540 or No. 543 Pots up to the 12" size. The 15" size will fit our Stock No. 150 Bowl and No. 103 - 15" Ring Jardiniere, No. 157 - 15" Biltmore Jardiniere and No. 101 - 15" Italian Pot.

STOCK No. 543
PINNACLE POT

SIZE	EACH
5"	$ .50
6"	.65
7"	.90
8"	1.10
10"	1.65
12"	2.50

SPECKLED COLORS: Lime Green, Grey, Pink, Oyster White Turquoise, Yellow.

ALSO MADE IN SOLID COLORS: Green, Yellow, Chartreuse,

STOCK No. 106
SAUCER

SIZE	EACH
3"	$ .17
4"	.22
5"	.33
6"	.40
7"	.55
8"	.65
9"	.85
10"	1.00
12"	1.40
14"	2.20

SOLID COLORS:
Olive Green, Yellow White, Chartreuse, Black

SPECKLED COLORS: Lime Green, Grey, Oyster White, Turquoise, Yellow, Pink.

J. A. BAUER POTTERY CO.

STOCK No. 149
LOW BOWL

SIZE	EACH
15"	$2.75

STOCK No. 150
BOWL

SIZE	EACH
15"	$2.75

STOCK No. 545
NEW LOW POT
TO FIT FERN PANS

SIZE	EACH
5½"	$ .55
7"	.70
8"	.95
9"	1.25
10"	1.65

SPECKLED COLORS ONLY:
Lime Green, Grey, Pink,
Oyster White

STOCK No. 204
SPANISH POT

SIZE	EACH
3" Spanish Pot	$ .18
4" Spanish Pot	.30
5" Spanish Pot	.45
6" Spanish Pot	.60
7" Spanish Pot	.85
8" Spanish Pot	1.00

SPECKLED COLORS ONLY
Lime green, Turquoise,
Oyster White, Pink, Gray, Yellow.

STOCK No. 551
SQUARE POT

SIZE	EACH
5"	$ .55
6"	.85
7"	1.10
8"	1.65

STOCK No. 157
BILTMORE JARDINIERE

SIZE	EACH
11"	$2.50
13"	3.50
15"	5.00

*STOCK No. 103
RING JARDINIERE

SIZE	EACH
11"	$2.50
13"	3.50
15"	5.00

STOCK No. 101
ROLLED RIM ITALIAN POT

SIZE	EACH
9"	$1.55
11"	2.75
13"	3.85
15"	5.50

STOCK No. 541
SWIRL JARDINIERE

SIZE	EACH
5" opening	$ .55
6" opening	.65
7" opening	.80

☆☆STOCK No. 122
SAND JAR

SIZE	EACH
9" x 20"	$5.50

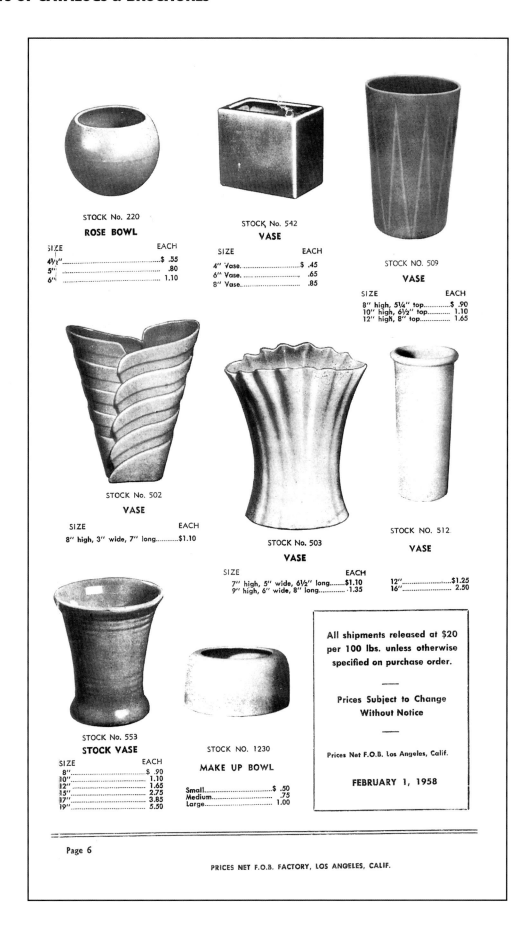

STOCK No. 220
ROSE BOWL

SIZE	EACH
4½"	$ .55
5"	.80
6"	1.10

STOCK No. 542
VASE

SIZE	EACH
4" Vase	$ .45
6" Vase	.65
8" Vase	.85

STOCK NO. 509
VASE

SIZE	EACH
8" high, 5¼" top	$ .90
10" high, 6½" top	1.10
12" high, 8" top	1.65

STOCK No. 502
VASE

SIZE	EACH
8" high, 3" wide, 7" long	$1.10

STOCK No. 503
VASE

SIZE	EACH
7" high, 5" wide, 6½" long	$1.10
9" high, 6" wide, 8" long	1.35

STOCK NO. 512
VASE

12"	$1.25
16"	2.50

STOCK NO. 553
STOCK VASE

SIZE	EACH
8"	$ .90
10"	1.10
12"	1.65
15"	2.75
17"	3.85
19"	5.50

STOCK NO. 1230
MAKE UP BOWL

Small	$ .50
Medium	.75
Large	1.00

All shipments released at $20 per 100 lbs. unless otherwise specified on purchase order.

———

Prices Subject to Change Without Notice

———

Prices Net F.O.B. Los Angeles, Calif.

FEBRUARY 1, 1958

PRICES NET F.O.B. FACTORY, LOS ANGELES, CALIF.

Kitchenware
and Other Items
by
J. A. Bauer Pottery Co.

415-421 West Avenue 33 • Los Angeles 31 California
Telephone: CApitol 5-4204

Originators and Manufacturers of
CALIFORNIA COLORED POTTERY

NET PRICE LIST—FEBRUARY 1958

New York Showroom • 261 Fifth Ave. • New York 16, New York

817—6-cup TEA
POT............$1.10 each
Speckled and Solid Colors

818—2-cup TEA
POT...........55c each
Speckled & Solid Colors

819—10-oz. MUG
................35c each
Speckled & Solid Colors

857—2-qt. BATTER
BOWL............................$1.10 each
Speckled Colors Only

858—1-quart BEATER
PITCHER............................85c each
Speckled Colors Only

Effective February 1958

Prices Net F.O.B. Factory,
Los Angeles, California

All shipments are released at $20.00
per 100 lbs., unless otherwise specified
on purchase order.

No Allowance for
Freight or Breakage
Prices Subject to Change
Without Notice

859—1-pint PITCHER................55c each
859—1-quart PITCHER..............80c each
859—2-quart PITCHER..........$1.35 each
859—2½-quart PITCHER........$1.65 each
Speckled Colors Only

Page 1

SPECKLED COLORS: Lime Green, Cocoa Brown, Lemon Yellow, Turquoise Blue,
Grey, Pink.
SOLID COLORS: Chartreuse, Olive Green, Dark Brown, Yellow, Burgundy.

850—6-piece MIXING BOWL SET
No. 9 to No. 36..........$3.75 set

850—5-piece MIXING BOWL
SET - Deep. No. 12 to
No. 36.....................$2.50 set

850—4-piece MIXING BOWL
SET - Deep. No. 18 to
No. 36.....................$1.65 set

Carton Pack 10c

Assorted Speckled Colors in each set

46—8-oz. MUG
.....................28c each
Speckled & Solid Colors

**87—COFFEE SERVER
WOOD HANDLE**
..............$1.65 each
Speckled & Solid Colors

406—SALAD BOWLS
7" diameter, 2" deep......55c each
8½" diameter, 2½"
deep.............................70c each
10" diameter, 3" deep....95c each
Speckled and Solid Color

806—SALAD BOWLS
7" diameter, 2" deep......55c each
8½" diameter, 2" deep..70c each
10½" diameter, 2" deep..95c each
13" diameter, 3½" deep
..................................$1.90 each
Speckled and Solid Colors

80—MIXING BOWLS   EACH

No. 36—5" (1-pt.).......................28c
No. 30—6" (1½-pt.).....................33c
No. 24—7½" (1-qt.).....................45c
No. 18—8½" (1½-qt.)...................55c
No. 12—9½" (3-qt.).....................65c
No. 9—10½" (4-qt.).....................90c
6-piece SET.............................$3.16
**Solid Colors Only in each size:
Chartreuse, Olive Green, Yellow**

847—REFRIGERATOR
3-piece SET................$1.10 set
Speckled Colors

J. A. BAUER POTTERY CO.
415-421 W. Ave. 33 · Los Angeles 31, Calif. · CApitol 5- 4204
PRICES NET F.O.B. FACTORY, LOS ANGELES, CALIF.

**LEAF—SALAD, FRUIT
or FLOWER BOWL**
644—9" diameter..........................$1.10
645—11" diameter........................$1.65
646—12½" diameter....................$2.20

686—HORS D'OEUVRES
13 in..$2.20

666—WESTERN HAT ASHTRAY
6 in.. .55

667—MEXICAN HAT ASHTRAY
6 in.. .55

212—SQUARE ASHTRAY
5"... .55
7".. .85
11"..$1.10

890—SNACK SET
Plate......................................$1.10
Mug.. .40

**889—HEART SALAD FRUIT
or FLOWER BOWL**
10"...$1.10
13"...$1.90

149—15" Low PLAIN SALAD BOWL
5 in Deep..................$2.75 each

148—15" BOWL—7½" Deep.........$3.85
Three Speckled Colors Only
Green, White, Pink

No. 3—15 in. PLAIN BOWL
Solid Yellow Only..............$2.75 each

All above items—speckled colors only—except #3

455—1-qt. CASSEROLE and COVER
....95c each

**455—1-qt. BRASS FINISH FRAME
or 1-qt. COPPER**...................95c each

**455—1½-qt. CASSEROLE
and COVER**.......................$1.40 each

**455—1½-qt. BRASS FINISH FRAME
or 1½-qt. COPPER**............$1.00 each

**455—2-qt. CASSEROLE and
COVER**...............................$1.65 each

**455—2-qt. BRASS FINISH FRAME
or 2-qt. COPPER**................$1.10 each

Carton Pk. 10c Extra

Speckled and Solid Colors

820—BUFFETS

Single with frame	$3.85
Double with frame	6.60
Single buffet warmer	4.95
Double buffet warmer	7.15

Speckled Colors

Packed in individual cartons when requested
at no extra charge.

**463—OVAL BAKER & FRAME
1½-qt.**.....................................$2.50

**Speckled Colors
Indiv. Carton Packed**................ .10

**457—1-qt. FOOD WARMER
COMPLETE**..........................$3.00 each
**457—1½-qt. FOOD WARMER,
COMPLETE**..........................$3.50 each
**457—2-qt. FOOD WARMER,
COMPLETE**..........................$4.00 each

Packed in individual cartons at no extra
charge.

Speckled and Solid Colors

425—1½-qt. FRENCH FOOD WARMER
...........................$3.50 each
425—2-qt. FRENCH FOOD WARMER
...........................$4.00 each

Speckled and Solid Colors

Packed in individual cartons at no extra
charge.

Page 4

SPECKLED COLORS: Lime Green, Cocoa Brown, Lemon Yellow, Turquoise Blue,
Grey, Pink.

SOLID COLORS: Chartreuse, Olive Green, Dark Brown, Yellow, Burgundy.

460—10" PIE PLATE................................85c each
460—10" BRASS FINISH FRAME........$1.00 each
Speckled Colors

603—COFFEE WARMER
complete...........................$2.20

Carton packed 10c extra

Speckled Colors

458

14" LAZY SUSAN, 4 TRAYS,
6" COVERED BOWL....................$4.50

882—RELISH DISH
10 inch.............................. .80

458

17" LAZY SUSAN, 4 TRAYS,
and 1-qt. CASSEROLE and COVER........$5.50 each

462—BEAN POT
1½ qt......................................$1.35

Speckled Colors

458

19" LAZY SUSAN, 6 TRAYS,
and 2-qt. CASSEROLE and COVER........$8.25 each

LAZY SUSANS carton packed 35c extra.

SUSANS made in speckled and Solid Colors.

BEAN POTS — Brown only

1-quart.......................65c each
2-quart.......................85c each
3-quart.......................$1.10 each
4-quart.......................$1.40 each

Page 5   **J. A. BAUER POTTERY CO.**
415-421 W. Ave. 33 • Los Angeles 31, Calif. • CApitol 5- 4204
PRICES NET F.O.B. FACTORY, LOS ANGELES, CALIF.

604—SUGAR BOWL..... .55   605—CREAM PITCHER.......... .55   891—NUT or CANDY BASKET
7 in................................... .95

461—JUMBO SALT or PEPPER
...........................70c each

Speckled and Solid Colors

832—SQUARE SALT or PEPPER
...........................55c each

609—PELICAN PITCHER
20 oz......................... .85

821C—FISH
Cookie Jar....................$2.20

822C—JUG
Cookie Jar....................$1.65

823C—SWIRL
Cookie Jar....................$1.65

814C—CHURN
Cookie Jar....................$2.20

815C—CANDY
Cookie Jar....................$2.20

816C—HEXAGON
Cookie Jar....................$2.20

(All above items made in speckled colors only unless otherwise marked)

Page 6

Prices Subject to Change
Without Notice

| SLATE | CHAMPAGNE WHITE | DESERT BEIGE | INDIO BROWN | PUMPKIN | SPICY GREEN |

CONTEMPO by *Brusché*

*Designed to fit the modern way of life in exciting California
colors. Contempo is earthenware that likes the oven.
And, to add practicality to beauty and versatility, Contempo's
new satin finish is fade, chip and scratch resistant.
Six color-harmonized hues that mix or match. Contempo
brings the fun and feel of California living to any table
setting. What more could be said for any dinnerware?*

```
                    CONTEMPO  DINNERWARE
                         · · · ···
                  J. A. BAUER  POTTERY  COMPANY

2633 Artesian Street --- Phone: CApitol 5-4204 --- Los Angeles 31, California

                         January 1, 1962

Sixteen piece starter set, carton packed, consisting of 4 cups and
saucers, 4 ten-inch dinner plates, 4 7-inch salad or luncheon plates.
Shipping weight 13½ lbs. . . . . . . . . . . . . . . . . . . . . . . . $ 6.00 net

Bulk  . . . . . . . . . . . . . . . . . . . . . . . . . . . . . . . . .    5.75 net

Forty-Five piece set, carton packed, consisting of 8 cups and saucers,
8 ten-inch dinner plates, 8 seven-inch salad or luncheon plates, 8 soup
or cereal, 1 creamer, and 1 sugar, 1 12-inch platter, 1 large vegetable.
Shipping weight 38 lbs. . . . . . . . . . . . . . . . . . . . . . .$ 17.50 net
```

Stock No.	Size	Description	Price
700		Cup only - 6 oz.	$ .35
700A		Saucer only	.25
701	10"	Dinner Plate	.65
702	7"	Luncheon or Salad Plate	.40
703	6"	Bread and Butter Plate	.30
704	5"	Fruit or Dessert	.25
705	5¼"	Deep Soup or Cereal	.40
706	10¼"	Platter	.85
707	12"	Platter	1.05
708	7½"	Vegetable Bowl	.65
709	9¼"	Vegetable Bowl	1.05
710		Covered Butter Dish	1.05
711		Creamer	.65
712		Covered Sugar Bowl	.75
712A		Covered Only	.15
713		Salt and Pepper	.65 Pr.
714	13"	Chop Plate	1.50
715		Gravy Boat	1.50
717	6 cup	Tea Pot	1.75
720	12 oz.	Handle Mug	.60
721	8 oz.	Handle Mug	.40
722	2 qt.	Ice Lip Pitcher	1.75
723	8 cup	Coffee Server	1.75
727	13"	Salad Bowl	1.90
729		Individual French Casserole Covered	.85
730	7½"	Round Vegetable or Serving Bowl	.80
731	9½"	Round Vegetable or Serving Bowl	1.05
732	½ Pt.	Pitcher	.65
732	1 Pt.	Pitcher	.75
732	1 Qt.	Pitcher	.95

```
COLORS:   Indio Brown, Desert Beige, Pumpkin, Champagne White and Spicy Green.

PLEASE NOTE:
     All dinnerware prices in this brochure are NET and therefore not subject to
quantity discounts.

     All prices quoted are F. O. B. FACTORY, LOS ANGELES, CALIFORNIA

     PRICES SUBJECT TO CHANGE WITHOUT NOTICE - - NO ALLOWANCE FOR FREIGHT OR
     BREAKAGE.
```

KITCHENWARE BY BAUER

*At last modern beauty has been added to utility in
        Kitchenware. Individual pieces or style-matched sets that
eliminate the "hodge-podge" look. A selection of finishes
        including the new Satin finish that likes the oven . . . it's fade,
chip and scratch resistant too. Gay colors, decorator colors . . .
        Bauer has them all.*

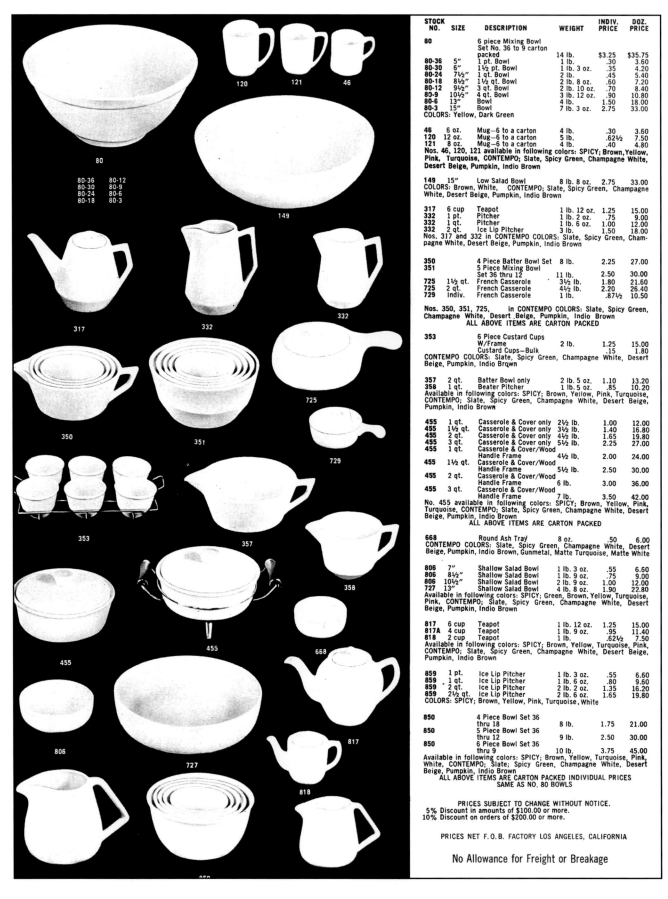

STOCK NO.	SIZE	DESCRIPTION	WEIGHT	INDIV. PRICE	DOZ. PRICE
80		6 piece Mixing Bowl Set No. 36 to 9 carton packed	14 lb.	$3.25	$35.75
80-36	5"	1 pt. Bowl	1 lb.	.30	3.60
80-30	6"	1½ pt. Bowl	1 lb. 3 oz.	.35	4.20
80-24	7½"	1 qt. Bowl	2 lb.	.45	5.40
80-18	8½"	1½ qt. Bowl	2 lb. 8 oz.	.60	7.20
80-12	9½"	3 qt. Bowl	2 lb. 10 oz.	.70	8.40
80-9	10½"	4 qt. Bowl	3 lb. 12 oz.	.90	10.80
80-6	13"	Bowl	4 lb.	1.50	18.00
80-3	15"	Bowl	7 lb. 3 oz.	2.75	33.00

COLORS: Yellow, Dark Green

STOCK NO.	SIZE	DESCRIPTION	WEIGHT	INDIV. PRICE	DOZ. PRICE
46	6 oz.	Mug—6 to a carton	4 lb.	.30	3.60
120	12 oz.	Mug—6 to a carton	5 lb.	.62½	7.50
121	8 oz.	Mug—6 to a carton	4 lb.	.40	4.80

Nos. 46, 120, 121 available in following colors: SPICY; Brown, Yellow, Pink, Turquoise, CONTEMPO; Slate, Spicy Green, Champagne White, Desert Beige, Pumpkin, Indio Brown

STOCK NO.	SIZE	DESCRIPTION	WEIGHT	INDIV. PRICE	DOZ. PRICE
149	15"	Low Salad Bowl	8 lb. 8 oz.	2.75	33.00

COLORS: Brown, White, CONTEMPO; Slate, Spicy Green, Champagne White, Desert Beige, Pumpkin, Indio Brown

STOCK NO.	SIZE	DESCRIPTION	WEIGHT	INDIV. PRICE	DOZ. PRICE
317	6 cup	Teapot	1 lb. 12 oz.	1.25	15.00
332	1 pt.	Pitcher	1 lb. 2 oz.	.75	9.00
332	1 qt.	Pitcher	1 lb. 6 oz.	1.00	12.00
332	2 qt.	Ice Lip Pitcher	3 lb.	1.50	18.00

Nos. 317 and 332 in CONTEMPO COLORS: Slate, Spicy Green, Champagne White, Desert Beige, Pumpkin, Indio Brown

STOCK NO.	SIZE	DESCRIPTION	WEIGHT	INDIV. PRICE	DOZ. PRICE
350		4 Piece Batter Bowl Set	8 lb.	2.25	27.00
351		5 Piece Mixing Bowl Set 36 thru 12	11 lb.	2.50	30.00
725	1½ qt.	French Casserole	3½ lb.	1.80	21.60
725	2 qt.	French Casserole	4½ lb.	2.20	26.40
729	Indiv.	French Casserole	1 lb.	.87½	10.50

Nos. 350, 351, 725, in CONTEMPO COLORS: Slate, Spicy Green, Champagne White, Desert Beige, Pumpkin, Indio Brown
ALL ABOVE ITEMS ARE CARTON PACKED

STOCK NO.	SIZE	DESCRIPTION	WEIGHT	INDIV. PRICE	DOZ. PRICE
353		6 Piece Custard Cups W/Frame	2 lb.	1.25	15.00
		Custard Cups—Bulk		.15	1.80

CONTEMPO COLORS: Slate, Spicy Green, Champagne White, Desert Beige, Pumpkin, Indio Brown

STOCK NO.	SIZE	DESCRIPTION	WEIGHT	INDIV. PRICE	DOZ. PRICE
357	2 qt.	Batter Bowl only	2 lb. 5 oz.	1.10	13.20
358	1 qt.	Beater Pitcher	1 lb. 5 oz.	.85	10.20

Available in following colors: SPICY; Brown, Yellow, Pink, Turquoise, CONTEMPO; Slate, Spicy Green, Champagne White, Desert Beige, Pumpkin, Indio Brown

STOCK NO.	SIZE	DESCRIPTION	WEIGHT	INDIV. PRICE	DOZ. PRICE
455	1 qt.	Casserole & Cover only	2½ lb.	1.00	12.00
455	1½ qt.	Casserole & Cover only	3½ lb.	1.40	16.80
455	2 qt.	Casserole & Cover only	4½ lb.	1.65	19.80
455	3 qt.	Casserole & Cover only	5½ lb.	2.25	27.00
455	1 qt.	Casserole & Cover/Wood Handle Frame	4½ lb.	2.00	24.00
455	1½ qt.	Casserole & Cover/Wood Handle Frame	5½ lb.	2.50	30.00
455	2 qt.	Casserole & Cover/Wood Handle Frame	6 lb.	3.00	36.00
455	3 qt.	Casserole & Cover/Wood Handle Frame	7 lb.	3.50	42.00

No. 455 available in following colors: SPICY; Brown, Yellow, Pink, Turquoise, CONTEMPO; Slate, Spicy Green, Champagne White, Desert Beige, Pumpkin, Indio Brown
ALL ABOVE ITEMS ARE CARTON PACKED

STOCK NO.	SIZE	DESCRIPTION	WEIGHT	INDIV. PRICE	DOZ. PRICE
668		Round Ash Tray	8 oz.	.50	6.00

CONTEMPO COLORS: Slate, Spicy Green, Champagne White, Desert Beige, Pumpkin, Indio Brown, Gunmetal, Matte Turquoise, Matte White

STOCK NO.	SIZE	DESCRIPTION	WEIGHT	INDIV. PRICE	DOZ. PRICE
806	7"	Shallow Salad Bowl	1 lb. 3 oz.	.55	6.60
806	8½"	Shallow Salad Bowl	1 lb. 9 oz.	.75	9.00
806	10½"	Shallow Salad Bowl	2 lb. 9 oz.	1.00	12.00
727	13"	Shallow Salad Bowl	4 lb. 8 oz.	1.90	22.80

Available in following colors: SPICY; Green, Brown, Yellow, Turquoise, Pink, CONTEMPO; Slate, Spicy Green, Champagne White, Desert Beige, Pumpkin, Indio Brown

STOCK NO.	SIZE	DESCRIPTION	WEIGHT	INDIV. PRICE	DOZ. PRICE
817	6 cup	Teapot	1 lb. 12 oz.	1.25	15.00
817A	4 cup	Teapot	1 lb. 9 oz.	.95	11.40
818	2 cup	Teapot	1 lb.	.62½	7.50

Available in following colors: SPICY; Brown, Yellow, Turquoise, Pink, CONTEMPO; Slate, Spicy Green, Champagne White, Desert Beige, Pumpkin, Indio Brown

STOCK NO.	SIZE	DESCRIPTION	WEIGHT	INDIV. PRICE	DOZ. PRICE
859	1 pt.	Ice Lip Pitcher	1 lb. 3 oz.	.55	6.60
859	1 qt.	Ice Lip Pitcher	1 lb. 6 oz.	.80	9.60
859	2 qt.	Ice Lip Pitcher	2 lb. 2 oz.	1.35	16.20
859	2½ qt.	Ice Lip Pitcher	2 lb. 6 oz.	1.65	19.80

COLORS: SPICY; Brown, Yellow, Pink, Turquoise, White

STOCK NO.	SIZE	DESCRIPTION	WEIGHT	INDIV. PRICE	DOZ. PRICE
850		4 Piece Bowl Set 36 thru 18	8 lb.	1.75	21.00
850		5 Piece Bowl Set 36 thru 12	9 lb.	2.50	30.00
850		6 Piece Bowl Set 36 thru 9	10 lb.	3.75	45.00

Available in following colors: SPICY; Brown, Yellow, Turquoise, Pink, White, CONTEMPO; Slate; Spicy Green, Champagne White, Desert Beige, Pumpkin, Indio Brown
ALL ABOVE ITEMS ARE CARTON PACKED INDIVIDUAL PRICES SAME AS NO. 80 BOWLS

PRICES SUBJECT TO CHANGE WITHOUT NOTICE.
5% Discount in amounts of $100.00 or more.
10% Discount on orders of $200.00 or more.

PRICES NET F.O.B. FACTORY LOS ANGELES, CALIFORNIA

No Allowance for Freight or Breakage

| SLATE | CHAMPAGNE WHITE | DESERT BEIGE | INDIO BROWN | PUMPKIN | SPICY GREEN |

"Moonsong" by Bauer

A fine blending of Contemporary and Oriental design that becomes unsurpassed casual beauty. At home in the oven or with any table setting, "Moonsong" is available in fifteen pieces, all in the new Satin Finish that makes fading, chipping and scratching a thing of the past. Soft color elegance in your choice of: Pumpkin, Spicy Green, Desert Beige, Indio Brown, Champagne White and Slate.

OVEN SERVEWARE

J. A. BAUER POTTERY COMPANY

PRICE LIST of OVEN SERVEWARE

Effective - - January 1, 1962

Stock No.	Size	Description		Price (Indiv.)
1100	16½"	COVERED CHIP & DIP	$	3.50
1101		INDIVIDUAL CASSEROLE & COVER or SUGAR		.85
1102		CREAMER		.85
1103		COFFEE SERVER & COVER with WARMER & WALNUT LEGS		3.75
1105		SERVING TRAY		1.75
1106	1 Qt.	COVERED CASSEROLE & FRAME with WALNUT LEGS & HANDLES		2.50
1106T		TWIN 1 QT. CASSEROLE & WARMER with WALNUT LEGS & HANDLES		5.00
1107	2½ Qt.	COVERED CASSEROLE & FRAME with WALNUT LEGS & HANDLES		3.50
1108	3 Qt.	COVERED CASSEROLE ONLY		3.50
1109	7½"	INDIVIDUAL SALAD BOWL		.60
1110	15"	SALAD BOWL		2.75
1111C	15"	CHIP & DIP SET		3.75
1111	7½"	INDIVIDUAL CHIP & DIP SET and FRAME (not illustrated.		1.75

COLORS: PUMPKIN, SPICY GREEN, DESERT BEIGE, INDIO BROWN, CHAMPAGNE WHITE and SLATE.

PRICES SUBJECT TO CHANGE WITHOUT NOTICE. 10% DISCOUNT ON ORDERS OF $200.00 OR MORE.

PRICES NET F. O. B. FACTORY, LOS ANGELES, CALIFORNIA AND SUBJECT TO CHANGE WITHOUT NOTICE.

NO ALLOWANCE FOR FREIGHT OR BREAKAGE.

J. A. BAUER POTTERY CO.

2633 ARTESIAN STREET • LOS ANGELES 31, CALIFORNIA • CAPITOL 5-4204

– PRICE LIST JANUARY 1962 –

FLORIST & GARDENWARE

SINCE 1885

BAUER POTTERY

California ORIGINATORS & MANUFACTORS OF COLORED POTTERY

"Everything for the Garden"

J. A. BAUER POTTERY CO.

CLAY PRODUCTS

2633 ARTESIAN STREET • LOS ANGELES 31, CALIFORNIA

#101 ROLLED RIM POT

11 inch	11 lbs.	3.00
13 inch	20 lbs.	4.00
15 inch	28 lbs.	5.75

COLORS: SPECK
—White, Brown
COLORS: GLOSS
—Black, Green, White

#103 RING JARDINERE

11 inch	14 lbs.	3.00
13 inch	17 lbs.	4.00
15 inch	27 lbs.	5.75

COLORS: GLOSS
—Green, Yellow, White, Black

#106 SAUCER

3 inch	4 oz.	.20 ea.
4 inch	8 oz.	.25 ea.
5 inch	8 oz.	.35 ea.
6 inch	12 oz.	.45 ea.
7 inch	14 oz.	.60 ea.
8 inch	1 lb. 4 oz.	.70 ea.
9 inch	2 lbs.	.90 ea.
10 inch	2 lb. 8 oz.	1.25 ea.
12 inch	3 lb. 8 oz.	1.50 ea.
14 inch	4 lb. 8 oz.	2.35 ea.

COLORS: SPECK
—White, Yellow, Turq., Brown, Pink
COLORS: GLOSS
—Yellow, White, Black, Green

#106A SAUCER for #1240

8 inch	1 lb. 4 oz.	.70 ea.
9 inch	2 lb.	.90 ea.
10 inch	2 lb. 8 oz.	1.25 ea.
12 inch	3 lb. 8 oz.	1.50 ea.

COLORS: MATTE
—Green, Beige, Black, Turq, White

#122 SAND JAR

10x20 inch   22 lbs.   5.75
COLORS: SPECK
—Yellow, White, Brown
COLORS: GLOSS
—Green, Yellow, Black

#124 SWIRL SAND JAR

10x18 inch   22 lbs.   5.75
COLORS: SPECK
—Yellow, White, Brown
COLORS: GLOSS
—Green, Yellow, Black

#126 BIRD BATH

18x23 inch   20 lbs.   7.75
COLORS: SPECK
—White, Yellow
Turq, Brown, Pink
COLORS: GLOSS
Green, Yellow

#129 OIL JAR

16 inch	15 lbs.	6.00
20 inch	20 lbs.	10.00

COLORS: SPECK
—Yellow, Turq, White

#146 INDIAN BOWL

7½ inch	2 lb. 10 oz.	.90 ea.
10 inch	3 lb. 13 oz.	1.75 ea.

COLORS: MATTE
—Green, Beige, Black, White

#147 FLOWER BOWL

13 inch   3 lb. 2 oz.   1.65 ea.
COLORS: MATTE
—Black, Green, White

#148 BOWL

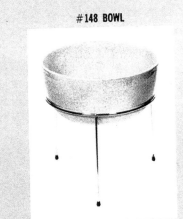

15x7½ inch .... 9 lbs.   4.00
Stand (brass) 1.50
COLORS: SPECK
—White, Brown

#149 LOW BOWL

15 inch .... 8 lbs.   3.00
COLORS: SPECK
—White, Brown

#150 BOWL

15 inch ....11 lb. 8 oz.   3.00
COLORS: GLOSS
—Green
COLORS: SPECK
—White

#157 BILTMORE JARDINERE

9 inch ....10 lbs.   1.50
11 inch ....14 lbs.   3.00
13 inch ....17 lbs.   4.00
15 inch ....25 lbs.   5.75
COLORS: SPECK
—White, Yellow
COLORS: GLOSS
—Black, Green

#505 VASE   #506 VASE

8 inch   8 oz. $1.00 ea.   8 inch 12 oz.   1.00 ea.
COLORS: SPECK
—Pink, White

#511 VASE

4½ inch .... 5 oz.   .30 ea.
9 inch .... 1 lb. 13 oz.   .75 ea.
COLORS: MATTE
—Green, Beige, Black, White

#513 PUMPKIN BOWL

6 inch ....1 lb. 4 oz.   .50 ea.
8 inch ....2 lb. 3 oz.   1.00 ea.
10 inch ....4 lbs.   1.50 ea.
COLORS: MATTE
—Green, Beige, Black, White

#514 HALF PUMPKIN BOWL

8 inch ...... 1 lb. 10 oz.   .70 ea.
10 inch ...... 3 lb. 2 oz.   1.25 ea.
COLORS: MATTE
—Green, Beige, Black, White

#516 VASE

6 inch ...... 1 lb. 12 oz. $ .75 ea.
8 inch ...... 2 lbs.   .90 ea.
10 inch ...... 2 lb. 5 oz.   1.10 ea.
COLORS: MATTE
—Green, Beige, Black, White,

#521-522 COMBINATION PEDESTAL POT

11&13 inch ....13 lbs. 4.25 pr.
13&15 inch ....20 lbs. 5.25 pr.
COLORS: MATTE
—Green, Beige, Black, White.

#522 DOUBLE PEDESTAL POT

11 inch ....15 lbs. 4.00 pr.
13 inch ....20 lbs. 5.50 pr.
COLORS: MATTE
—Green, Beige, Black, White.

#543 DOUBLE PINNACLE POT

10 inch ....15 lbs. 3.50 ea.
12 inch ....22 lbs. 5.00 ea.
COLORS: MATTE
—Green, Beige, Black, White

#520 BOAT BOWL

16 inch ....1 lb. 10 oz. .75 ea.
20 inch ....2 lb. 12 oz. 1.50 ea.
COLORS: MATTE
—Green, Beige, Black, White,

#521 BOWL

13 inch ....5 lb. 3 oz. 2.25 ea.
15 inch ....10 lb.s. 3.00 ea.
COLORS: MATTE
—Green, Beige, Black, White,

#523 LONG BOWL

18 inch .... 3 lb. 12 oz. 2.50 ea.
COLORS: MATTE
—Green, Beige, Black, White,

522 #PEDESTAL POT

11 inch .... 7 lbs. 2.00 ea.
13 inch .... 9 lb. 7 oz. 2.75 ea.
COLORS: MATTE
—Green, Beige, Black, White.

#525 COMPOTE

8 inch .... 4 lbs. 1.25 ea.
10¼ inch ...... 8 lbs. 1.75 ea.
COLORS: MATTE
—Green, Beige, Black, White.

#526 BOWL

15 inch .... 1 lb. 2.00 ea.

#527 CANDLE HOLDERS

8 oz. .... .75 pr.
COLORS: MATTE
—Green, Beige, Black, White

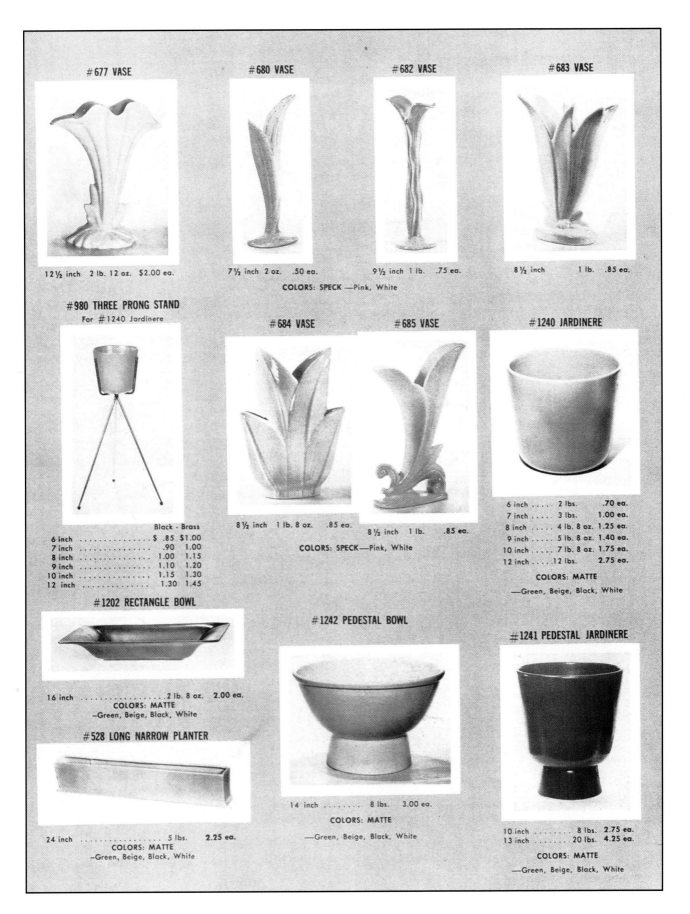

#677 VASE

12½ inch   2 lb. 12 oz. $2.00 ea.

#680 VASE

7½ inch 2 oz.   .50 ea.

#682 VASE

9½ inch 1 lb.   .75 ea.

COLORS: SPECK —Pink, White

#683 VASE

8½ inch   1 lb.   .85 ea.

#980 THREE PRONG STAND
For #1240 Jardinere

#684 VASE

8½ inch   1 lb. 8 oz.   .85 ea.

#685 VASE

8½ inch   1 lb.   .85 ea.

COLORS: SPECK—Pink, White

#1240 JARDINERE

6 inch . . . . .   2 lbs.   .70 ea.
7 inch . . . . .   3 lbs.   1.00 ea.
8 inch . . . . .   4 lb. 8 oz. 1.25 ea.
9 inch . . . . .   5 lb. 8 oz. 1.40 ea.
10 inch . . . .   7 lb. 8 oz. 1.75 ea.
12 inch . . . . .12 lbs.   2.75 ea.

COLORS: MATTE
—Green, Beige, Black, White

	Black	Brass
6 inch	$ .85	$1.00
7 inch	.90	1.00
8 inch	1.00	1.15
9 inch	1.10	1.20
10 inch	1.15	1.30
12 inch	1.30	1.45

#1202 RECTANGLE BOWL

16 inch . . . . .2 lb. 8 oz. 2.00 ea.
COLORS: MATTE
—Green, Beige, Black, White

#1242 PEDESTAL BOWL

14 inch . . . . 8 lbs.   3.00 ea.
COLORS: MATTE
—Green, Beige, Black, White

#1241 PEDESTAL JARDINERE

10 inch . . . . 8 lbs. 2.75 ea.
13 inch . . . . 20 lbs. 4.25 ea.
COLORS: MATTE
—Green, Beige, Black, White

#528 LONG NARROW PLANTER

24 inch . . . . 5 lbs.   2.25 ea.
COLORS: MATTE
—Green, Beige, Black, White

#534 FLOWER BOWL

9 inch . . . . 1 lb. 4 oz. .80 ea.

COLORS: MATTE
—Green, Beige, Black, White

#530 GRECIAN VASE

16 inch High x 11 inch Dia.
7 lb. 8 oz. . . . . . 5.50 ea.

COLORS: MATTE
—Black, White

#532 ROUND LOW FLOWER BOWL

10 inch . . . . . . 1 lb. 14 oz. .80 ea.

COLORS: MATTE
—Green, Beige, Black, White

#536 LONG FLOWER BOWL

12 inch . . . . 1 lb. 8 oz. .80 ea.

COLORS: MATTE
—Green, Beige, Black, White

#545 VIOLET POT/FAST SAUCER

5 ½ inch . . . . . . 2 lb.   1.00 ea.

COLORS: MATTE
—Green, Beige, Black, White

#540 SWIRL POTS

3 inch	8 oz.	$ .20 ea.
4 inch	12 oz.	.35 ea.
5 inch	1 lb. 8 oz.	.50 ea.
6 inch	2 lbs.	.65 ea.
7 inch	4 lbs.	.90 ea.
8 inch	5 lbs.	1.10 ea.
10 inch	7 lbs.	1.65 ea.
12 inch	10 lbs.	2.50 ea.

COLORS: GLOSS
—Green, Black, White

COLORS: SPECK
—White, Yellow, Turq., Brown, Pink

#543 PINNACLE POT

5 inch	1 lb. 12 oz.	.50 ea.
6 inch	2 lb. 8 oz.	.65 ea.
7 inch	3 lb. 12 oz.	.90 ea.
8 inch	5 lb. 4 oz.	1.10 ea.
10 inch	7 lb. 8 oz.	1.65 ea.
12 inch	11 lbs.	2.50 ea.

COLORS: SPECK
—White, Turq, Yellow, Brown, Pink

#880 RING STAND

	Black	Brass
6 inch	$ .85	$ .85
7 inch	.85	1.00
8 inch	.85	1.10
10 inch	.90	1.15
12 inch	1.05	1.25
15 inch	1.15	1.30

For #540-#543 up to 12 inch
#150-#103-#157-#101 15 inch use 15 inch ring

#546 DOMEPOT

9 inch	4 lbs.	2.00 ea.
Stand	1 lb. 8 oz.	1.15 ea.
11 inch	7 lbs.	3.00 ea.
Stand	1 lb. 8 oz.	1.20 ea.
14 inch	15 lbs.	4.00 ea.
Stand	2 lb. 8 oz.	1.35 ea.

COLORS: SPECK
—Brown, Turq, White
COLORS: MATTE
—Black

#545A — LOW POT

5 ½ inch . . . . 1 lb. 8 oz.   .60 ea.

COLORS: MATTE
—Pink, White, Green
not illustrated

#553 STOCK VASE

8 inch	2 lbs.	1.00 ea.
10 inch	4 lbs.	1.25 ea.
12 inch	7 lbs.	1.75 ea.
15 inch	10 lbs.	2.00 ea.
17 inch	12 lbs.	4.00 ea.
19 inch	15 lbs.	5.75 ea.

COLORS: SPECK
—White, Brown
COLORS: GLOSS
—Black, White, Green

TERRA COTTA GARDEN WARE

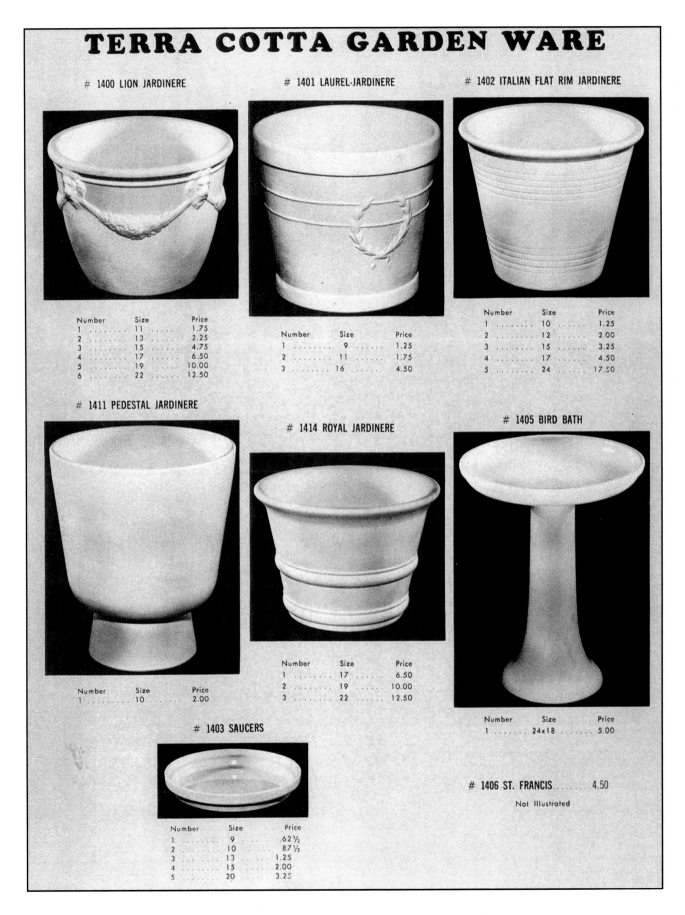

1400 LION JARDINERE

Number	Size	Price
1	11	1.75
2	13	2.25
3	15	4.75
4	17	6.50
5	19	10.00
6	22	12.50

1401 LAUREL-JARDINERE

Number	Size	Price
1	9	1.25
2	11	1.75
3	16	4.50

1402 ITALIAN FLAT RIM JARDINERE

Number	Size	Price
1	10	1.25
2	12	2.00
3	15	3.25
4	17	4.50
5	24	17.50

1411 PEDESTAL JARDINERE

Number	Size	Price
1	10	2.00

1414 ROYAL JARDINERE

Number	Size	Price
1	17	6.50
2	19	10.00
3	22	12.50

1405 BIRD BATH

Number	Size	Price
1	24x18	5.00

1406 ST. FRANCIS 4.50

Not Illustrated

1403 SAUCERS

Number	Size	Price
1	9	.62½
2	10	.87½
3	13	1.25
4	15	2.00
5	20	3.25

RED CLAY FLOWER POTS

PRICES EFFECTIVE JANUARY 1, 1962

RED CLAY FLOWER POTS

		Each
2	Inch	$ .02
2¼	Inch	.03
2½	Inch	.04
3	Inch	.05
4	Inch	.08
5	Inch	.12
6	Inch	.15
7	Inch	.22
8	Inch	.35
9	Inch	.65
10	Inch	.90
12	Inch	1.75

RED CLAY FERN PANS

		Each
4	Inch	$ .08
5	Inch	.12
6	Inch	.15
7	Inch	.22
8	Inch	.35
9	Inch	.65
10	Inch	.90
12	Inch	1.75

HANGING BASKETS

8	Inch	.80
9	Inch	.90
10	Inch	1.35

ROLLED RIM POTS

		Each
8	Inch	$1.00
10	Inch	1.45
12	Inch	2.00
14	Inch	3.00

FLOWER POT SAUCERS

4	Inch	.10
5	Inch	.15
6	Inch	.18
7	Inch	.25
8	Inch	.30
9	Inch	.45
10	Inch	.60
12	Inch	1.00
14	Inch	1.50

No Allowance for Freight or Breakage

Prices F.O.B. Factory

Subject to packing charge if packed for shipping

J. A. Bauer Pottery Co.

2633 ARTESIAN STREET • LOS ANGELES 31, CALIFORNIA

CApitol 5-4204

PRICE LIST

GARDENWARE — **JAN. 1961**

Number	Size	Description	Weight	Old Price	New Price
#101	11 inch	Rolled Rim Pot	11 lbs.	$2.75	$2.50 ea.
	13 inch	Rolled Rim Pot	20 lbs.	3.85	3.50 ea.
	15 inch	Rolled Rim Pot	28 lbs.	5.50	5.00 ea.
		COLORS: SPECK—Green, White, Brown; GLOSS—Black, White			
#103	11 inch	Ring Jardinere	14 lbs.		2.50 ea.
	13 inch	Ring Jardinere	17 lbs.		3.50 ea.
	15 inch	Ring Jardinere	27 lbs.		5.00 ea.
		COLORS: GLOSS—Green, Yellow, White, Black			
#106	3 inch	Saucers	4 oz.		.17 ea.
	4 inch	Saucers	8 oz.		.22 ea.
	5 inch	Saucers	8 oz.		.33 ea.
	6 inch	Saucers	12 oz.		.40 ea.
	7 inch	Saucers	14 oz.		.55 ea.
	8 inch	Saucers	1 lb. 4 oz.		.65 ea.
	9 inch	Saucers	2 lbs.		.85 ea.
	10 inch	Saucers	2 lb. 8 oz.		1.00 ea.
	12 inch	Saucers	3 lb. 8 oz.		1.40 ea.
	14 inch	Saucers	4 lb. 8 oz.		2.20 ea.
		COLORS: SPECK—Green, White, Turq, Yellow, Pink, Brown; GLOSS—Yellow, White, Black			
#106A For #1240	8 inch	Saucers	1 lb. 4 oz.		.65 ea.
	9 inch	Saucers	2 lb.		.85 ea.
	10 inch	Saucers	2 lb. 8 oz.		1.00 ea.
	12 inch	Saucers	3 lb. 8 oz.		1.40 ea.
		COLORS: MATTE—Green, Beige, Black, Turq, White, Pink, Yellow			
#122	9x20 inch	Sand Jar	22 lbs.		5.50 ea.
		COLORS: GLOSS—Green, Yellow, Black, Royal Blue; SPECK—Brown, Green, Yellow, White			
#124	9x18 inch	Swirl Sand Jar	22 lbs.		5.50 ea.
		COLORS: GLOSS—Green, Yellow, Black, Royal Blue; SPECK—Green, Yellow, White, Brown			
#126	18x23 inch	Bird Bath	20 lbs.	8.00	6.00 ea.
		COLORS: GLOSS—Green, White, Yellow; SPECK—Green, Yellow			
#129	16 inch	Oil Jar	15 lbs.	5.00	4.50 ea.
	20 inch	Oil Jar	20 lbs.	10.00	8.00 ea.
		COLORS: GLOSS—Yellow, Dark Blue; SPECK—Green, Yellow, Turq, White, Pink			
#146G	7½ inch	Indian Bowl	2 lb. 10 oz.		.80 ea.
	10 inch	Indian Bowl	3 lb. 13 oz.		1.50 ea.
		COLORS: MATTE—Green, Beige, Black, White, Turq, Pink; GOLD DECORATION			
#147	13 inch	Flower Bowl	3 lb. 2 oz.		$1.50 ea.
		COLORS: MATTE—Black, Green, White; SPECK—Green, Pink, White, Yellow, Brown, Turq			
#148	15x7½ inch	Bowl	9 lbs.	$3.85	3.75 ea.
		Stand (brass)		1.75	1.30 ea.
		COLORS: SPECK—Green, White, Brown			
#149	15 inch	Low Bowl	8 lbs.	2.75	2.50 ea.
		COLORS: SPECK—Green, White, Brown			
#150	15 inch	Bowl	11 lb. 8 oz.	2.75	2.50 ea.
		COLORS: MATTE—Black; SPECK—Green, White, Yellow			

Page 1

J. A. Bauer Pottery Co.

2633 ARTESIAN STREET • LOS ANGELES 31, CALIFORNIA

CApitol 5-4204

PRICE LIST

GARDENWARE — **JAN. 1961**

Number	Size	Description	Weight	Old Price	New Price
#157	11 inch	Biltmore Jardinere	14 lbs.		2.50 ea.
	13 inch	Biltmore Jardinere	17 lbs.		3.50 ea.
	15 inch	Biltmore Jardinere	25 lbs.		5.00 ea.
		SPECK—Green, White, Yellow			
#220	4½ inch	Rose Bowl	1 lb.	.55	.40 ea.
	5 inch	Rose Bowl	1 lb. 12 oz.	.80	.60 ea.
	6 inch	Rose Bowl	2 lb. 4 oz.	1.10	.80 ea.
		COLORS: SPECK—Green, White, Brown			
#505G	8 inch	Vase	8 oz.		$1.00 ea.
#506G	8 inch	Vase	12 oz.		1.00 ea.
		COLORS: SPECK—Green, Pink, White; GOLD DECORATION			
#509	8 inch	Tall Pinnacle Vase	2 lb. 4 oz.		.90 ea.
	10 inch	Tall Pinnacle Vase	4 lbs.		1.10 ea.
	12 inch	Tall Pinnacle Vase	8 lbs.		1.65 ea.
		COLORS: MATTE—Green, Beige, Black, Turq, White, Yellow			
#511	4½ inch	Vase	5 oz.		.30 ea.
	9 inch	Vase	1 lb. 13 oz.		.75 ea.
		COLORS: MATTE—Green, Beige, Black, Turq, White, Yellow			
#512	12 inch	Tall Vase	3 lb. 12 oz.		1.25 ea.
	16 inch	Tall Vase	7 lbs.		2.50 ea.
		COLORS: SPECK—Green, White, Brown			
#513G	6 inch	Pumpkin Bowl	1 lb. 4 oz.	.40	.50 ea.
	8 inch	Pumpkin Bowl	2 lb. 3 oz.	.80	1.00 ea.
	10 inch	Pumpkin Bowl	4 lbs.	1.25	1.60 ea.
		COLORS: MATTE—Green, Beige, Black, Turq, White, Yellow; GOLD DECORATION			
#514	8 inch	Half Pumpkin Bowl	1 lb. 10 oz.		.60 ea.
	10 inch	Half Pumpkin Bowl	3 lb. 2 oz.		1.10 ea.
		COLORS: MATTE—Green, Beige, Black, Turq, White, Yellow			
#516	6 inch	Vase	1 lb. 12 oz.		$ .75 ea.
	8 inch	Vase	2 lbs.		.90 ea.
	10 inch	Vase	2 lb. 5 oz.		1.10 ea.
		COLORS: MATTE—Green, Beige, Black, White, Turq, Yellow			
#517	6 inch	Bowl	1 lb.		.45 ea.
	7 inch	Bowl	1 lb. 6 oz.		.60 ea.
	8 inch	Bowl	1 lb. 15 oz.		.75 ea.
	9 inch	Bowl	2 lb. 4 oz.		.90 ea.
		COLORS: MATTE—Green, Beige, Black, White, Turq, Yellow			
#520	16 inch	Boat Bowl	1 lb. 10 oz.		.75 ea.
	20 inch	Boat Bowl	2 lb. 12 oz.		1.50 ea.
		COLORS: MATTE—Green, Beige, Black, Turq, White, Yellow			
#520G	16 inch	Boat Bowl	1 lb. 10 oz.		1.00 ea.
	20 inch	Boat Bowl	2 lb. 12 oz.		2.00 ea.
		COLORS: MATTE—Green, Beige, Black, Turq, White, Yellow; GOLD DECORATION			
#520T	16 inch	Two Tone Boat Bowl	1 lb. 10 oz.		1.00 ea.
	20 inch	Two Tone Boat Bowl	2 lb. 12 oz.		2.00 ea.
		COLORS:			
#521	13 inch	Bowl	5 lb. 3 oz.		2.00 ea.
	15 inch	Bowl	10 lb.s.		2.75 ea.
		COLORS: MATTE—Green, Beige, Black, Turq, White, Yellow			
#522	11 inch	Pedestal Pot	7 lbs.		1.75 ea.
	13 inch	Pedestal Pot	9 lb. 7 oz.		2.50 ea.
		COLORS: MATTE—Green, Beige, Black, Turq, White, Yellow			

Page 2

J. A. Bauer Pottery Co.

2633 ARTESIAN STREET • LOS ANGELES 31, CALIFORNIA

CApitol 5-4204

PRICE LIST

GARDENWARE — **JAN. 1961**

Number	Size	Description	Weight	Old Price	New Price
#522	11 inch	Double Pedestal Pot	15 lbs.		3.50 pr.
	13 inch	Double Pedestal Pot	20 lbs.		5.00 pr.
		COLORS: MATTE—Green, Beige, Black, Turq, White, Yellow			
#521-522	11&13 inch	Double Pedestal Pot	13 lbs.		3.75 pr.
	13&15 inch	Double Pedestal Pot	20 lbs.		5.25 pr.
		COLORS: MATTE—Green, Beige, Black, Turq, White, Yellow			
#523	18 inch	Long Bowl	3 lb. 12 oz.		2.50 ea.
		COLORS: MATTE—Green, Beige, Black, Turq, White, Yellow			
#524	18 inch	Deep Round Bowl	5 lb. 9 oz.		3.50 ea.
		COLORS: MATTE—Green, Beige, Black, Turq, White, Yellow			
#525G	8 inch	Compote	4 lbs.		1.00 ea.
	10¼ inch	Compote	8 lbs.		1.50 ea.
		COLORS: MATTE—Green, Beige, Black, Turq, White, Yellow; GOLD DECORATION			
#526	15 inch	Bowl	1 lb.		2.00 ea.
#527		Candle Holders	8 oz.		.75 pr.
		COLORS: MATTE—Green, Beige, Black, White, Yellow			
#530		Glecian Vase	7 lb. 8 oz.		5.00 ea.
		COLORS: MATTE—Black, White			
#532	10 inch	Round Low Flower Bowl	1 lb. 14 oz.		.75 ea.
		COLORS: MATTE—Green, Beige, Black, White, Yellow			
#534	9 inch	Flower Bowl	1 lb. 4 oz.		.75 ea.
		COLORS: MATTE—Green, Beige, Black, White, Yellow			
#536	12 inch	Long Flower Bowl	1 lb. 8 oz.		.75 ea.
		COLORS: MATTE—Green, Beige, Black, White, Yellow			
#540	3 inch	Swirl Pots	8 oz.		$ .20 ea.
	4 inch	Swirl Pots	12 oz.		.35 ea.
	5 inch	Swirl Pots	1 lb. 8 oz.		.50 ea.
	6 inch	Swirl Pots	2 lbs.		.65 ea.
	7 inch	Swirl Pots	4 lbs.		.90 ea.
	8 inch	Swirl Pots	5 lbs.		1.10 ea.
	10 inch	Swirl Pots	7 lbs.		1.65 ea.
	12 inch	Swirl Pots	10 lbs.		2.50 ea.
		COLORS: GLOSS—Green, White, Black, Royal Blue; SPECK—Green, Pink, White, Turq, Yellow, Brown			
#542	4 inch	Square Vase	12 oz.		.45 ea.
	6 inch	Square Vase	1 lb.		.65 ea.
	8 inch	Square Vase	2 lbs.		.80 ea.
		COLORS: SPECK—Green, White, Brown; MATTE—Black, White			
#543	5 inch	Pinnacle Pot	1 lb. 12 oz.		.50 ea.
	6 inch	Pinnacle Pot	2 lb. 8 oz.		.65 ea.
	7 inch	Pinnacle Pot	3 lb. 12 oz.		.90 ea.
	8 inch	Pinnacle Pot	5 lb. 4 oz.		1.10 ea.
	10 inch	Pinnacle Pot	7 lb. 8 oz.		1.65 ea.
	12 inch	Pinnacle Pot	11 lbs.		2.50 ea.
		COLORS: SPECK—Green, White, Turq, Yellow, Brown			
#545	5½ inch	Low Fern Pot	1 lb.	$ .55	.50 ea.
	7½ inch	Low Fern Pot	2 lb. 8 oz.	.70	.75 ea.
		COLORS: SPECK—Green, White, Brown			

Page 3

J. A. Bauer Pottery Co.

2633 ARTESIAN STREET • LOS ANGELES 31, CALIFORNIA

CApitol 5-4204

PRICE LIST

GARDENWARE — **JAN. 1961**

Number	Size	Description	Weight	Old Price	New Price
#546	9 inch	Dome Pot	4 lbs.	2.20	2.00 ea.
		Stand (black only)	1 lb. 8 oz.	1.55	1.15 ea.
	11 inch	Dome Pot	7 lbs.	3.30	3.00 ea.
		Stand (black only)	1 lb. 8 oz.	1.65	1.20 ea.
	14 inch	Dome Pot	15 lbs.	4.90	4.00 ea.
		Stand (black only)	2 lb. 8 oz.	2.20	1.55 ea.
		COLORS: SPECK—Green, Brown, Turq, White; MATTE—Black, White			
#552	9 inch	Oblong Planter	1 lb. 15 oz.		1.00 ea.
	12 inch	Oblong Planter	2 lbs.		1.50 ea.
		COLORS: MATTE—Green, Black, White, Yellow			
#553	8 inch	Stock Vase	2 lbs.		.90 ea.
	10 inch	Stock Vase	4 lbs.		1.10 ea.
	12 inch	Stock Vase	7 lbs.		1.65 ea.
	15 inch	Stock Vase	10 lbs.		2.75 ea.
	17 inch	Stock Vase	12 lbs.	3.85	3.25 ea.
	19 inch	Stock Vase	15 lbs.	5.50	5.00 ea.
		COLORS: SPECK—Green, White, Brown; MATTE—Black, White			
#677G	12½ inch	Vase	2 lb. 12 oz.		$2.00 ea.
		COLORS: SPECK—Green, Pink, White; GOLD DECORATION			
#680G	7½ inch	Vase	2 oz.		.50 ea.
#682G	9½ inch	Vase	1 lb.		.75 ea.
#683G	8½ inch	Vase	1 lb.		.85 ea.
#684G	8½ inch	Vase	1 lb. 8 oz.		.85 ea.
#685G	8½ inch		1 lb.		.85 ea.
		COLORS: SPECK—Green, Pink, White; GOLD DECORATION		Black - Brass	Black - Brass
#880	6 inch	Ring Stand		$1.10 $1.10	$ .85 $ .85
	7 inch	Ring Stand		1.10 1.35	.85 1.00
	8 inch	Ring Stand		1.10 1.45	.85 1.10
	10 inch	Ring Stand		1.20 1.55	.90 1.15
	12 inch	Ring Stand		1.40 1.65	1.05 1.25
	15 inch	Ring Stand		1.55 1.75	1.15 1.30
		For #540-#543 up to 12 inch; #150-#103-#157-#101 15 inch use 15 inch ring			
#980	6 inch	Three Prong Stand		$1.10 $1.30	$ .85 $1.00
	7 inch	Three Prong Stand		1.20 1.35	.90 1.00
	8 inch	Three Prong Stand		1.30 1.35	1.00 1.15
	9 inch	Three Prong Stand		1.45 1.65	1.10 1.20
	10 inch	Three Prong Stand		1.55 1.75	1.15 1.30
		For #1240			
#1202	16 inch	Rectangle Bowl	2 lb. 8 oz.	1.50	2.00 ea.
		COLORS: MATTE—Green, Beige, Black, Turq, White, Yellow			
#1240	8 inch	Jardinere	4 lb. 8 oz.		1.10 ea.
	9 inch	Jardinere	5 lb. 8 oz.		1.35 ea.
	10 inch	Jardinere	7 lb. 8 oz.		1.65 ea.
	12 inch	Jardinere	12 lbs.		2.50 ea.
		COLORS: MATTE—Green, Black, Beige, Turq, White, Yellow			
#1241	12 inch	Bowl	8 lbs.		2.00 ea.
		COLORS: MATTE—Green, Black, Beige, Turq, White, Yellow			
#1242	8½ inch	Bowl	8 lbs.		2.00 ea.
		COLORS: MATTE—Green, Beige, Black, Turq, White, Yellow			

Page 4

J. A. Bauer Pottery Co.

2633 ARTESIAN STREET • LOS ANGELES 31, CALIFORNIA

CApitol 5-4204

PRICE LIST
KITCHENWARE AND ARTWARE

JAN. 1961

Number	Size	Description	Weight	Old Price	New Price
#3	15 inch	Bowl	7 lb. 3 oz.	$2.75	$2.50 ea.
		COLOR: GLOSS—Yellow only			
#6	13 inch	Bowl	4 lbs.		1.50 ea.
		COLOR: GLOSS—Yellow only			
#46	8 oz.	Mug (6 ctn. pk.)	4 lbs. ctn.	.28	3.00 dz.
		COLORS: SPECK—Green, Brown, Yellow, Turq, Pink, White			
		GLOSS—Yellow, Green, Burgundy			
#80	Set	Mixing Bowls (6 ctn. pk.)	14 lbs. ctn.	3.26	36.00 dz.
#80-36	5 inch	1 pt. Bowl	1 lb.	.28	3.00 dz.
#80-30	6 inch	1½ pt. Bowl	1 lb. 3 oz.	.33	3.60 dz.
#80-24	7½ inch	1 qt. Bowl	2 lbs.	.45	4.80 dz.
#80-18	8½ inch	1½ qt. Bowl	2 lb. 8 oz.		6.60 dz.
#80-12	9½ inch	3 qt. Bowl	2 lb. 10 oz.	.68	7.80 dz.
#80- 9	10½ inch	4 qt. Bowl	3 lb. 12 oz.	.90	10.20 dz.
		COLORS: GLOSS—Chart, Green, Yellow			
#149	15 inch	Low Salad Bowl	8 lb. 8 oz.	2.75	30.00 dz.
		COLORS: SPECK—Green, White, Brown			
#212G	5 inch	Ash Tray	10 oz.		6.00 dz.
	7 inch	Ash Tray	1 lb. 2 oz.		9.00 dz.
	11 inch	Ash Tray	2 lb. 8 oz.		12.00 dz.
		COLORS: MATTE—Green, Beige, Black, Turq, White, Yellow			
		GOLD DECORATION			
#300	Set	4 pc. Batter Bowl			27.00 dz.
		COLORS: SPECK—Green, Brown, Yellow, Turq, White			
#455	1 qt.	Casserole*Frame (ctn. pk.)	6 lbs.	2.00	21.00 dz.
	1½ qt.	Casserole*Frame (ctn. pk.)	8 lbs.	2.50	27.00 dz.
	2 qt.	Casserole*Frame (ctn. pk.)	9 lbs.	2.85	30.00 dz.
	3 qt.	Casserole*Frame (ctn. pk.)	11 lbs.	3.50	36.00 dz.
#455A	1 qt.	Casserole Only	2 lb. 4 oz.	.95	10.80 dz.
	1½ qt.	Casserole Only	3 lb. 2 oz.	1.40	15.00 dz.
	2 qt.	Casserole Only	3 lb. 10 oz.	1.65	18.00 dz.
	3 qt.	Casserole Only	4 lb. 13 oz.	2.25	24.00 dz.
		COLORS: SPECK—White, Brown, Yellow, Pink			
		GLOSS—White Bottom			
		COVER—Green, Blue, Sand			
#463	1½ qt.	Oval Baker*Frame (ctn. pk.)	6 lbs.	2.50	27.00 dz.
	2 qt.	Oval Baker*Frame (ctn. pk.)	8 lbs.		36.00 dz.
#463A	1½ qt.	Oval Baker Only	2 lbs.	1.40	15.00 dz.
	2 qt.	Oval Baker Only	3 lbs.	1.65	18.00 dz.
		COLORS: Same as Casseroles			
#645G	11 inch	Salad Bowl, Leaf	3 lb. 3 oz.	1.65	24.00 dz.
		COLORS: SPECK—Green, Brown, Yellow, White			
		GOLD DECORATION			
#668		Ash Tray, Round	8 oz.	.50	6.00 oz.
		Colors: Matte-Green-Black-Beige-Turq-White-Yellow			

Page 1

J. A. Bauer Pottery Co.

2633 ARTESIAN STREET • LOS ANGELES 31, CALIFORNIA

CApitol 5-4204

PRICE LIST
KITCHENWARE AND ARTWARE

JAN. 1961

Number	Size	Description	Weight	Old Price	New Price
#686G	13 inch	Hors D'oeuvres		$2.20	$30.00 dz.
		COLORS: SPECK—Green, Yellow, Brown, White			
		GOLD DECORATION			
#806	7 inch	Shallow Salad Bowl	1 lb. 3 oz.	.55	6.00 dz.
	8½ inch	Shallow Salad Bowl	1 lb. 9 oz.	.75	9.00 dz.
	10½ inch	Shallow Salad Bowl	2 lb. 9 oz.	.95	10.80 dz.
	13 inch	Shallow Salad Bowl	4 lb. 10 oz.	1.90	21.00 dz.
		COLORS: SPECK—Green, Brown, Yellow, Turq			
		GLOSS—Green, Yellow			
#850	Set	3 pc. Bowl 12-24-36 (ctn. pk.)	7 lbs.	1.75	18.00 dz.
	Set	4 pc. Bowl 18 thru 36	8 lbs.	1.75	18.00 dz.
	Set	5 pc. Bowl 12 thru 36	9 lbs.	2.50	27.00 dz.
	Set	6 pc. Bowl 9 thru 36	10 lbs.	3.75	36.00 dz.
		COLORS: SPECK—Green, Brown, Yellow, Turq, Pink, Blue			
		Individual Prices Same As #80			
#817	6 cup	Teapot	1 lb. 12 oz.		13.20 dz.
#817A	4 cup	Teapot	1 lb. 9 oz.		10.20 dz.
#818	2 cup	Teapot	1 lb.	.55	6.00 dz.
		COLORS: SPECK—Green, Brown, Yellow, Turq, Pink, White			
#819	10 oz.	Mug (ctn. pk. 6)	2 lbs. ctn.	.35	4.80 dz.
		COLORS: SPECK—Green, Brown, Yellow, Turq, Pink, White			
#857	2 qt.	Batter Bowl	2 lbs.	1.10	12.00 dz.
#858	1 qt.	Beater Pitcher	1 lb. 3 oz.	.85	9.00 dz.
		COLORS: SPECK—Green, Brown, Yellow, Turq, White			
#891	1 qt.	Bean Pot	9 oz.	.65	7.20 dz.
	2 qt.	Bean Pot		.85	10.80 dz.
	3 qt.	Bean Pot		1.10	12.00 dz.
	4 qt.	Bean Pot		1.40	18.00 dz.
		COLOR: Brown Only			

J. A. Bauer Pottery Co.

2633 ARTESIAN STREET • LOS ANGELES 31, CALIFORNIA

CApitol 5-4204

Manufacturers of

CLAY PRODUCTS   Net List

Beckman's Hi Grade Stoneware, Flower Pots, Garden Pottery and Art Pottery

This list supersedes all previous lists. Prices subject to change without notice.

RED CLAY FLOWER POTS

MACHINE MADE Flower Pots

	Per 1,000
2 Inch	$16.50
2¼ Inch	17.60
2½ Inch	18.70
3 Inch	19.80
4 Inch	38.50
5 Inch	60.50
5½ Inch	66.00
6 Inch	71.50
7 Inch	121.00
8 Inch	220.00

Quantities of 10M or more of a size, less 20%

FLOWER POTS

9 Inch	$ .55
10 Inch	.77
12 Inch	1.50

MACHINE MADE FERN POTS

	Per 1,000
4 Inch	$38.50
5 Inch	60.50
6 Inch	71.50
7 Inch	121.00
8 Inch	220.00

Quantities of 10M or more of a size, less 20%

FERN PANS

	Each
9 Inch	$ .55
10 Inch	.77

Pots—Rolled Rim

	Each
8 Inch	$ .75
10 Inch	1.00
12 Inch	1.50
14 Inch	2.50

HANGING BASKETS

	Each
8 Inch	$ .55
9 Inch	.85
10 Inch	1.10
Wires for Baskets	.22

FLOWER POT SAUCERS

	Each
4 Inch	$ .11
5 Inch	.13
6 Inch	.17
7 Inch	.22
8 Inch	.28
9 Inch	.39
10 Inch	.55
12 Inch	.94
14 Inch	1.38

NEW LAVA GLAZE POTS

LAVA POTS

3 Inch	$ .20
4 Inch	.22
5 Inch	.25
6 Inch	.30
7 Inch	.40
8 Inch	.65

LAVA SAUCERS

4 Inch	$ .30
5 Inch	.35
6 Inch	.50
7 Inch	.65

Colors: Charcoal, White, Pink, Light Blue, Light Green and Yellow.

No Allowance for Freight or Breakage • Prices F.O.B. Factory

Subject to packing charge if packed for shipping

Page 1

ABOUT THE AUTHOR

Over twenty years ago, Jack Chipman began collecting California ceramics. In time, Chipman had amassed a huge collection of the ceramics of his native state. This led to extensive research on the subject.

By the 1980s, Jack Chipman was an expert on California pottery, particularly Bauer pottery. In 1980, Chipman published *The Bauer Pottery Price Guide,* which he co-authored with Judy Stangler. This book was so popular that Jack was urged to publish a second book, *The Complete Collectors Guide to Bauer Pottery,* which was published in 1982 and co-authored by Judy Stangler.

Jack Chipman's research on California ceramics continued, and soon he was a known and respected authority on every aspect of California clayware. This knowledge culminated in the publication of a third book, *The Collector's Encyclopedia of California Pottery,* published in 1992 by Collector Books.

After the publication of his third book, Chipman was able to devote himself to his "other life." Few people in the world of collectible ceramics realize that Jack is also a talented fine artist whose work is in the collections of several museums. Vestiges of his years of involvement with ceramics come through in the textures and coloration of his paintings. His assemblages are a series of witty and sardonic one-liners aimed at topical issues of American culture.

As Chipman focused on his art, another book was being written on Bauer pottery. Mitch Tuchman put together an elegant volume on Bauer pottery for Chronicle Books and asked Jack to be a contributing writer. Chipman wrote the section on Bauer's late-period artware.

With the public's growing interest in Bauer pottery, Chipman felt the urgent demand, not only for an historical perspective on the colorful clayware, but also for an up-to-date comprehensive price guide; hence this book.

BIBLIOGRAPHY

BOOKS

Chipman, Jack. *Collector's Encyclopedia of California Pottery*. Paducah, KY: Collector Books, 1992.

Chipman, Jack; Judy Stangler. *Bauer Pottery 1980 Price Guide*. Culver City, CA: California Spectrum, 1980.

————. *The Complete Collectors Guide to Bauer Pottery*. Culver City, CA: California Spectrum, 1982.

————. *The Complete Collectors Guide to Bauer Pottery*. Stamford, CT: Jo-D Books, Revised Second Printing, 1986.

Duke, Harvey. *The Official Price Guide to Pottery and Porcelain, Eighth Edition*. New York: House of Collectibles, 1995.

Evans, Paul. *Art Pottery of the United States*. New York: Charles Scribner's Sons, 1974.

Hayes, Barbara Jean. *Bauer: The California Pottery Rainbow*. Venice, CA: Salem Witch Antiques, 1975.

————. *Bauer: The California Pottery Rainbow*. Venice, CA: Salem Witch Antiques, Revised Second Printing, 1979.

Kerr, Ann. *The Collector's Encyclopedia of Russel Wright Designs*, Paducah, KY: Collector Books, 1990.

Lehner, Lois. *Lehner's Enclycopedia of U.S. Marks On Pottery, Porcelain & Clay*. Paducah, KY: Collector Books, 1988.

Satchel, Ed; Pat Begrin. *J.A. Bauer Pottery Co.* Willows, CA: General Store, 1981.

Tuchman, Mitch. *Bauer: Classic American Pottery*. San Francisco: Chronicle Books, 1995.

Weaver, John B. *L.A. El Pueblo Grande*. Pasadena, CA: The Ward Ritchie Press, 1973.

EXHIBITION CATALOGS

Kent, Caroline. *Southern California Pottery*. Downey, CA: Downey Museum of Art, 1978.

Orlando, Philip, et al. *Pottery, 1880–1960*. Encino, CA: Orlando Gallery, 1973.

Pickel, Susan E. *From Kiln to Kitchen: American Ceramic Design in Tableware*. Springfield: Illinois State Museum, 1980.

Verlangieri, Michael. *Bauer Art Pottery*. Cambria, CA: Verlangieri Gallery, 1991.

Verlangieri, Michael. *Bauer Pottery: The Matt Carlton Years*. Cambria, CA: Verlangieri Gallery, 1992.

PERIODICALS

Anon. "California's Bright Bauer Ware." *American Collector*, October 1982, p. 46.

Anon. "Collections: Bauer." *Journal of the American Art Pottery Association*, January/February 1994, p. 19.

Baldinger, Scott. "Bauer Ware." *Martha Stewart Living*, May 1995, p. 64.

Chipman, Jack. "A Rainbow for Every Table." *The Antique Trader Weekly*, November 10, 1982, p. 66.

————. "The Coast's Own Colorful Collectible." *West Coast Peddler*, March 1992, p. 25.

Chipman, Jack; Judy Stangler. "A California Success Story, Part I: "Ringware and Other Dishes." *The Glaze*, May, 1980, p. 11.

————. "A California Success Story, Part II: Artware and Additional History." *The Glaze*, July 1980, p. 10.

Burstein, Joanne. "The Bauer Pottery." *American Ceramics: The Ceramic Art Quarterly*, Winter 1983, p. 44.

Grenier, Meridith. "Pots of Gold." *Santa Monica Outlook*, June 11, 1996, p. D3.

Johnson, Bruce E. "Bauer Pottery." *Country Living*, April 1996, p. 48.

Johnson, Elaine. "Plate Tectonics." *Sunset*, November 1996, p. 76.

Kerr, Ann. "Bauer & Russel Wright." *The Glaze*, December 1981, p. 9.

Reed, Rochelle. "California Sun Settings." *New West*, August 14, 1978, p. 68.

Sims, Judith. "California Collectibles." *Los Angeles Times Magazine*, January 5, 1992, p. 30.

Sroloff, Deborah. "Save Our State." *Los Angeles Magazine*, April 1989, p. 146.

Smith, Doris W. "Pretty & Practical Bauer Pottery." *The Antique Trader Weekly*, January 2, 1973, p. 32.

Stanton, D. M. "Bauer at the Wheel." *Journal of the American Art Pottery Association*, September/October 1989, p. 4.

Tuchman, Mitch. "Bauer: The Early Artwares." *Journal of the American Art Pottery Association*, November/December 1995, p. 8.

———. "Beauty and the Bisque." *Los Angeles Times Magazine*, December 3, 1995, p. 46.

Verlangieri, Michael. "The Matt Carlton Years at Bauer Pottery," *West Coast Peddler*, October 1992, p. 31.

NEWSLETTERS

Dozer, Dean, ed. *Bauer News, Vol. 1–6* and "Color Supplement." Pasadena, CA: Nocq Road Publications, 1994.

Lukaszewski, Tim; Paul Preston, eds. *Bauer Quarterly*, Berkeley, CA: 1996–ongoing.

REPRINTED BAUER CATALOGS

Chipman, Jack; Judy Stangler, eds. *Bauer 1941 California Pottery Catalog Reprint*. Culver City, CA: California Spectrum, 1981.

Tuchman, Mitch, ed. *High Grade Colored and Natural Finishes, J. A. Bauer Pottery Co.* n.d. Los Angeles: Verna Mae Press, 1992.

WEBSITES

The Russel Wright & Twentieth Century Modern Internet Chat Group.
http://www.netspace.org/cgi-bin/lwgate/Russel-Wright/

Collector Online.
http://www.collectoronline.com/collect

Michael Verlangieri.
http://www.thebook.com/verlangieri

INDEX

COLLECTOR BOOKS

Informing Today's Collector

For over two decades we have been keeping collectors informed on trends and values in all fields of antiques and collectibles.

DOLLS, FIGURES & TEDDY BEARS

4707	A Decade of **Barbie Dolls** & Collectibles, 1981–1991, Summers	$19.95
4631	**Barbie Doll** Boom, 1986–1995, Augustyniak	$18.95
2079	**Barbie Doll** Fashion, Volume I, Eames	$24.95
4846	**Barbie Doll** Fashion, Volume II, Eames	$24.95
3957	**Barbie** Exclusives, Rana	$18.95
4632	**Barbie** Exclusives, Book II, Rana	$18.95
5672	The **Barbie Doll** Years, 4th Ed., Olds	$19.95
3810	**Chatty Cathy** Dolls, Lewis	$15.95
5352	Collector's Ency. of **Barbie** Doll Exclusives & More, 2nd Ed.,Augustyniak	$24.95
2211	Collector's Encyclopedia of **Madame Alexander** Dolls, Smith	$24.95
4863	Collector's Encyclopedia of **Vogue Dolls**, Izen/Stover	$29.95
5821	**Doll Values**, Antique to Modern, 5th Ed., Moyer	$12.95
5829	**Madame Alexander** Collector's Dolls Price Guide #26, Crowsey	$12.95
5833	**Modern Collectible Dolls**, Volume V, Moyer	$24.95
5689	**Nippon Dolls** & Playthings, Van Patten/Lau	$29.95
5365	**Peanuts Collectibles**, Podley/Bang	$24.95
5253	Story of **Barbie**, 2nd Ed., Westenhouser	$24.95
5277	**Talking Toys** of the 20th Century, Lewis	$15.95
1513	**Teddy Bears & Steiff** Animals, Mandel	$9.95
1817	**Teddy Bears & Steiff** Animals, 2nd Series, Mandel	$19.95
2084	**Teddy Bears, Annalee's & Steiff** Animals, 3rd Series, Mandel	$19.95
5371	**Teddy Bear** Treasury, Yenke	$19.95
1808	Wonder of **Barbie**, Manos	$9.95
1430	World of **Barbie** Dolls, Manos	$9.95
4880	World of **Raggedy Ann** Collectibles, Avery	$24.95

TOYS, MARBLES & CHRISTMAS COLLECTIBLES

2333	Antique & Collectible **Marbles**, 3rd Ed., Grist	$9.95
5353	**Breyer Animal** Collector's Guide, 2nd Ed., Browell	$19.95
4976	**Christmas Ornaments**, Lights & Decorations, Johnson	$24.95
4737	**Christmas Ornaments**, Lights & Decorations, Vol. II, Johnson	$24.95
4739	**Christmas Ornaments**, Lights & Decorations, Vol. III, Johnson	$24.95
4559	Collectible **Action Figures**, 2nd Ed., Manos	$17.95
2338	Collector's Encyclopedia of **Disneyana**, Longest, Stern	$24.95
5038	Collector's Guide to **Diecast Toys** & Scale Models, 2nd Ed., Johnson	$19.95
4651	Collector's Guide to **Tinker Toys**, Strange	$18.95
4566	Collector's Guide to **Tootsietoys**, 2nd Ed., Richter	$19.95
5169	Collector's Guide to **TV Toys** & Memorabilia, 2nd Ed., Davis/Morgan	$24.95
5360	**Fisher-Price Toys**, Cassity	$19.95
4720	The Golden Age of **Automotive Toys**, 1925–1941, Hutchison/Johnson	$24.95
5593	Grist's Big Book of **Marbles**, 2nd Ed.	$24.95
3970	Grist's Machine-Made & Contemporary **Marbles**, 2nd Ed.	$9.95
5267	**Matchbox Toys**, 1947 to 1998, 3rd Ed., Johnson	$19.95
5830	**McDonald's** Collectibles, 2nd Edition, Henriques/DuVall	$24.95
5673	Modern **Candy Containers** & Novelties, Brush/Miller	$19.95
1540	Modern **Toys** 1930–1980, Baker	$19.95
3888	**Motorcycle Toys**, Antique & Contemporary, Gentry/Downs	$18.95
5693	**Schroeder's Collectible Toys**, Antique to Modern Price Guide, 7th Ed.	$17.95

FURNITURE

1457	American **Oak** Furniture, McNerney	$9.95
3716	American **Oak** Furniture, Book II, McNerney	$12.95
1118	Antique **Oak** Furniture, Hill	$7.95
2271	Collector's Encyclopedia of **American** Furniture, Vol. II, Swedberg	$24.95
3720	Collector's Encyclopedia of **American** Furniture, Vol. III, Swedberg	$24.95
5359	Early **American** Furniture, Obbard	$12.95
1755	Furniture of the **Depression Era**, Swedberg	$19.95
3906	**Heywood-Wakefield** Modern Furniture, Rouland	$18.95
1885	**Victorian** Furniture, Our American Heritage, McNerney	$9.95
3829	**Victorian** Furniture, Our American Heritage, Book II, McNerney	$9.95

JEWELRY, HATPINS, WATCHES & PURSES

1712	Antique & Collectible **Thimbles** & Accessories, Mathis	$19.95
1748	Antique **Purses**, Revised Second Ed., Holiner	$19.95
1278	Art Nouveau & Art Deco **Jewelry**, Baker	$9.95
4850	Collectible **Costume Jewelry**, Simonds	$24.95
5675	Collectible **Silver Jewelry**, Rezazadeh	$24.95
3722	Collector's Ency. of **Compacts**, Carryalls & Face Powder Boxes, Mueller	$24.95
4940	**Costume Jewelry**, A Practical Handbook & Value Guide, Rezazadeh	$24.95
1716	Fifty Years of Collectible **Fashion Jewelry**, 1925–1975, Baker	$19.95
1424	**Hatpins** & Hatpin Holders, Baker	$9.95
5695	**Ladies' Vintage Accessories**, Bruton	$24.95
1181	100 Years of Collectible **Jewelry**, 1850–1950, Baker	$9.95
4729	**Sewing Tools** & Trinkets, Thompson	$24.95
5620	Unsigned Beauties of **Costume Jewelry**, Brown	$24.95
4878	Vintage & Contemporary **Purse Accessories**, Gerson	$24.95
5696	Vintage & Vogue Ladies' **Compacts**, 2nd Edition, Gerson	$29.95

INDIANS, GUNS, KNIVES, TOOLS, PRIMITIVES

1868	Antique **Tools**, Our American Heritage, McNerney	$9.95
5616	Big Book of **Pocket Knives**, Stewart	$19.95
4943	Field Guide to Flint **Arrowheads & Knives** of the North American Indian	$9.95
2279	**Indian Artifacts** of the Midwest, Book I, Hothem	$14.95
3885	**Indian Artifacts** of the Midwest, Book II, Hothem	$16.95
4870	**Indian Artifacts** of the Midwest, Book III, Hothem	$18.95
5685	**Indian Artifacts** of the Midwest, Book IV, Hothem	$19.95
5687	**Modern Guns**, Identification & Values, 13th Ed., Quertermous	$14.95
2164	**Primitives**, Our American Heritage, McNerney	$9.95
1759	**Primitives**, Our American Heritage, 2nd Series, McNerney	$14.95
4730	Standard **Knife** Collector's Guide, 3rd Ed., Ritchie & Stewart	$12.95

PAPER COLLECTIBLES & BOOKS

4633	**Big Little Books**, Jacobs	$18.95
4710	Collector's Guide to **Children's Books**, 1850 to 1950, Volume I, Jones	$18.95
5153	Collector's Guide to **Children's Books**, 1850 to 1950, Volume II, Jones	$19.95
5596	Collector's Guide to **Children's Books**, 1950 to 1975, Volume III, Jones	$19.95
1441	Collector's Guide to **Post Cards**, Wood	$9.95
2081	Guide to Collecting **Cookbooks**, Allen	$14.95
5825	Huxford's **Old Book** Value Guide, 13th Ed.	$19.95
2080	Price Guide to **Cookbooks** & Recipe Leaflets, Dickinson	$9.95
3973	**Sheet Music** Reference & Price Guide, 2nd Ed., Pafik & Guiheen	$19.95
4654	**Victorian Trade Cards**, Historical Reference & Value Guide, Cheadle	$19.95
4733	**Whitman Juvenile Books**, Brown	$17.95

GLASSWARE

5602	Anchor Hocking's **Fire-King** & More, 2nd Ed.	$24.95
4561	Collectible **Drinking Glasses**, Chase & Kelly	$17.95
5823	Collectible **Glass Shoes**, 2nd Edition, Wheatley	$24.95
5357	Coll. **Glassware** from the 40s, 50s & 60s, 5th Ed., Florence	$19.95
1810	Collector's Encyclopedia of **American Art Glass**, Shuman	$29.95
5358	Collector's Encyclopedia of **Depression Glass**, 14th Ed., Florence	$19.95
1961	Collector's Encyclopedia of **Fry Glassware**, Fry Glass Society	$24.95
1664	Collector's Encyclopedia of **Heisey Glass**, 1925–1938, Bredehoft	$24.95
3905	Collector's Encyclopedia of **Milk Glass**, Newbound	$24.95
4936	Collector's Guide to **Candy Containers**, Dezso/Poirier	$19.95
4564	**Crackle Glass**, Weitman	$19.95
4941	**Crackle Glass**, Book II, Weitman	$19.95
4714	**Czechoslovakian Glass** and Collectibles, Book II, Barta/Rose	$16.95
5528	Early American **Pattern Glass**, Metz	$17.95
5682	**Elegant Glassware** of the Depression Era, 9th Ed., Florence	$19.95
5614	Field Guide to **Pattern Glass**, McCain	$17.95
3981	Evers' Standard **Cut Glass** Value Guide	$12.95
4659	**Fenton** Art Glass, 1907–1939, Whitmyer	$24.95
5615	Florence's **Glassware Pattern Identification** Guide, Vol. II	$19.95

COLLECTOR BOOKS
Informing Today's Collector

4719	**Fostoria**, Etched, Carved & Cut Designs, Vol. II, Kerr	$24.95
3883	**Fostoria Stemware**, The Crystal for America, Long/Seate	$24.95
5261	**Fostoria Tableware**, 1924 – 1943, Long/Seate	$24.95
5361	**Fostoria Tableware**, 1944 – 1986, Long/Seate	$24.95
5604	**Fostoria**, Useful & Ornamental, Long/Seate	$29.95
4644	**Imperial Carnival Glass**, Burns	$18.95
5827	**Kitchen Glassware** of the Depression Years, 6th Ed., Florence	$24.95
5600	Much More Early American **Pattern Glass**, Metz	$17.95
5690	Pocket Guide to **Depression Glass**, 12th Ed., Florence	$9.95
5594	Standard Encyclopedia of **Carnival Glass**, 7th Ed., Edwards/Carwile	$29.95
5595	Standard **Carnival Glass** Price Guide, 12th Ed., Edwards/Carwile	$9.95
5272	Standard Encyclopedia of **Opalescent Glass**, 3rd Ed., Edwards/Carwile	$24.95
5617	Standard Encyclopedia of **Pressed Glass**, 2nd Ed., Edwards/Carwile	$29.95
4731	**Stemware Identification**, Featuring Cordials with Values, Florence	$24.95
4732	**Very Rare Glassware** of the Depression Years, 5th Series, Florence	$24.95
4656	**Westmoreland Glass**, Wilson	$24.95

POTTERY

4927	**ABC Plates & Mugs**, Lindsay	$24.95
4929	**American Art Pottery**, Sigafoose	$24.95
4630	**American Limoges**, Limoges	$24.95
1312	**Blue & White Stoneware**, McNerney	$9.95
1958	So. Potteries **Blue Ridge Dinnerware**, 3rd Ed., Newbound	$14.95
1959	**Blue Willow**, 2nd Ed., Gaston	$14.95
4851	Collectible **Cups & Saucers**, Harran	$18.95
1373	Collector's Encyclopedia of **American Dinnerware**, Cunningham	$24.95
4931	Collector's Encyclopedia of **Bauer Pottery**, Chipman	$24.95
4932	Collector's Encyclopedia of **Blue Ridge Dinnerware**, Vol. II, Newbound	$24.95
4658	Collector's Encyclopedia of **Brush-McCoy Pottery**, Huxford	$24.95
5034	Collector's Encyclopedia of **California Pottery**, 2nd Ed., Chipman	$24.95
2133	Collector's Encyclopedia of **Cookie Jars**, Roerig	$24.95
3723	Collector's Encyclopedia of **Cookie Jars**, Book II, Roerig	$24.95
4939	Collector's Encyclopedia of **Cookie Jars**, Book III, Roerig	$24.95
5748	Collector's Encyclopedia of **Fiesta**, 9th Ed., Huxford	$24.95
4718	Collector's Encyclopedia of **Figural Planters & Vases**, Newbound	$19.95
3961	Collector's Encyclopedia of **Early Noritake**, Alden	$24.95
1439	Collector's Encyclopedia of **Flow Blue China**, Gaston	$19.95
3812	Collector's Encyclopedia of **Flow Blue China**, 2nd Ed., Gaston	$24.95
3431	Collector's Encyclopedia of **Homer Laughlin China**, Jasper	$24.95
1276	Collector's Encyclopedia of **Hull Pottery**, Roberts	$19.95
3962	Collector's Encyclopedia of **Lefton China**, DeLozier	$19.95
4855	Collector's Encyclopedia of **Lefton China**, Book II, DeLozier	$19.95
5609	Collector's Encyclopedia of **Limoges Porcelain**, 3rd Ed., Gaston	$29.95
2334	Collector's Encyclopedia of **Majolica Pottery**, Katz-Marks	$19.95
1358	Collector's Encyclopedia of **McCoy Pottery**, Huxford	$19.95
5677	Collector's Encyclopedia of **Niloak**, 2nd Edition, Gifford	$29.95
3837	Collector's Encyclopedia of **Nippon Porcelain**, Van Patten	$24.95
1665	Collector's Ency. of **Nippon Porcelain**, 3rd Series, Van Patten	$24.95
4712	Collector's Ency. of **Nippon Porcelain**, 4th Series, Van Patten	$24.95
5053	Collector's Ency. of **Nippon Porcelain**, 5th Series, Van Patten	$24.95
5678	Collector's Ency. of **Nippon Porcelain**, 6th Series, Van Patten	$29.95
1447	Collector's Encyclopedia of **Noritake**, Van Patten	$19.95
1038	Collector's Encyclopedia of **Occupied Japan**, 2nd Series, Florence	$14.95
4951	Collector's Encyclopedia of **Old Ivory China**, Hillman	$24.95
5564	Collector's Encyclopedia of **Pickard China**, Reed	$29.95
3877	Collector's Encyclopedia of **R.S. Prussia**, 4th Series, Gaston	$24.95
5679	Collector's Encyclopedia of **Red Wing Art Pottery**, Dollen	$24.95
5618	Collector's Encyclopedia of **Rosemeade Pottery**, Dommel	$24.95
5841	Collector's Encyclopedia of **Roseville Pottery**, Revised, Huxford/Nickel	$24.95
5842	Collector's Encyclopedia of **Roseville Pottery**, 2nd Series, Huxford/Nickel	$24.95
4713	Collector's Encyclopedia of **Salt Glaze Stoneware**, Taylor/Lowrance	$24.95
3314	Collector's Encyclopedia of **Van Briggle Art Pottery**, Sasicki	$24.95
4563	Collector's Encyclopedia of **Wall Pockets**, Newbound	$19.95
2111	Collector's Encyclopedia of **Weller Pottery**, Huxford	$29.95
5680	Collector's Guide to **Feather Edge Ware**, McAllister	$19.95
3876	Collector's Guide to **Lu-Ray Pastels**, Meehan	$18.95

3814	Collector's Guide to **Made in Japan Ceramics**, White	$18.95
4646	Collector's Guide to **Made in Japan Ceramics**, Book II, White	$18.95
2339	Collector's Guide to **Shawnee Pottery**, Vanderbilt	$19.95
1425	**Cookie Jars**, Westfall	$9.95
3440	**Cookie Jars**, Book II, Westfall	$19.95
4924	Figural & Novelty **Salt & Pepper Shakers**, 2nd Series, Davern	$24.95
2379	Lehner's Ency. of **U.S. Marks** on Pottery, Porcelain & China	$24.95
4722	**McCoy Pottery**, Collector's Reference & Value Guide, Hanson/Nissen	$19.95
5691	**Post86 Fiesta**, Identification & Value Guide, Racheter	$19.95
1670	**Red Wing Collectibles**, DePasquale	$9.95
1440	**Red Wing Stoneware**, DePasquale	$9.95
1632	**Salt & Pepper Shakers**, Guarnaccia	$9.95
5091	**Salt & Pepper Shakers** II, Guarnaccia	$18.95
3443	**Salt & Pepper Shakers** IV, Guarnaccia	$18.95
3738	**Shawnee Pottery**, Mangus	$24.95
4629	Turn of the Century **American Dinnerware**, 1880s–1920s, Jasper	$24.95
3327	**Watt Pottery** – Identification & Value Guide, Morris	$19.95

OTHER COLLECTIBLES

5838	Advertising **Thermometers**, Merritt	$16.95
4704	Antique & Collectible **Buttons**, Wisniewski	$19.95
2269	Antique **Brass & Copper** Collectibles, Gaston	$16.95
1880	Antique **Iron**, McNerney	$9.95
3872	Antique **Tins**, Dodge	$24.95
4845	Antique **Typewriters & Office Collectibles**, Rehr	$19.95
5607	Antiquing and Collecting on the **Internet**, Parry	$12.95
1128	**Bottle** Pricing Guide, 3rd Ed., Cleveland	$7.95
3718	Collectible **Aluminum**, Grist	$16.95
4560	Collectible **Cats**, An Identification & Value Guide, Book II, Fyke	$19.95
5060	Collectible **Souvenir Spoons**, Bednersh	$19.95
5676	Collectible **Souvenir Spoons**, Book II, Bednersh	$29.95
5666	Collector's Encyclopedia of **Granite Ware**, Book 2, Greguire	$29.95
5836	Collector's Guide to **Antique Radios**, 5th Ed., Bunis	$19.95
5608	Collector's Gde. to Buying, Selling & Trading on the **Internet**, 2nd Ed., Hix	$12.95
4637	Collector's Guide to **Cigarette Lighters**, Book I, Flanagan	$17.95
3966	Collector's Guide to **Inkwells**, Identification & Values, Badders	$18.95
4947	Collector's Guide to **Inkwells**, Book II, Badders	$19.95
5681	Collector's Guide to **Lunchboxes**, White	$19.95
5621	Collector's Guide to **Online Auctions**, Hix	$12.95
4862	Collector's Guide to **Toasters** & Accessories, Greguire	$19.95
4652	Collector's Guide to **Transistor Radios**, 2nd Ed., Bunis	$16.95
4864	Collector's Guide to **Wallace Nutting Pictures**, Ivankovich	$18.95
1629	**Doorstops**, Identification & Values, Bertoia	$9.95
5683	**Fishing Lure** Collectibles, 2nd Ed., Murphy/Edmisten	$29.95
5259	**Flea Market Trader**, 12th Ed., Huxford	$9.95
4945	**G-Men and FBI Toys** and Collectibles, Whitworth	$18.95
5605	**Garage Sale & Flea Market Annual**, 8th Ed.	$19.95
3819	**General Store** Collectibles, Wilson	$24.95
5159	Huxford's Collectible **Advertising**, 4th Ed.	$24.95
2216	**Kitchen Antiques**, 1790–1940, McNerney	$14.95
5686	**Lighting Fixtures** of the Depression Era, Book I, Thomas	$24.95
4950	The **Lone Ranger**, Collector's Reference & Value Guide, Felbinger	$18.95
2026	**Railroad** Collectibles, 4th Ed., Baker	$14.95
5619	**Roy Rogers and Dale Evans** Toys & Memorabilia, Coyle	$24.95
5692	**Schroeder's Antiques Price Guide**, 19th Ed., Huxford	$14.95
5007	**Silverplated Flatware**, Revised 4th Edition, Hagan	$18.95
5694	**Summers' Guide to Coca-Cola**, 3rd Ed.	$24.95
5356	**Summers' Pocket Guide to Coca-Cola**, 2nd Ed.	$9.95
3892	**Toy & Miniature Sewing Machines**, Thomas	$18.95
4876	**Toy & Miniature Sewing Machines**, Book II, Thomas	$24.95
5144	Value Guide to **Advertising Memorabilia**, 2nd Ed., Summers	$19.95
3977	Value Guide to **Gas Station Memorabilia**, Summers & Priddy	$24.95
4877	Vintage **Bar Ware**, Visakay	$24.95
4935	The **W.F. Cody Buffalo Bill** Collector's Guide with Values	$24.95
5281	**Wanted to Buy**, 7th Edition	$9.95

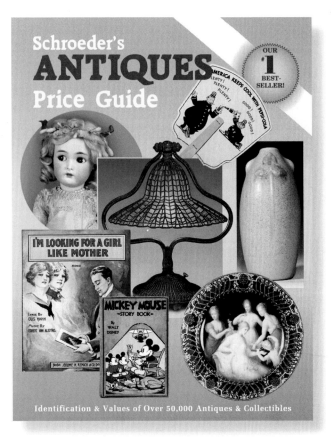